AS LAW FOR OCR

Jimmy O'Riordan

Heinemann Educational Publishers
Halley Court, Jordan Hill, Oxford OX2 8EJ
a division of Reed Educational & Professional Publishing Ltd

OXFORD   MELBOURNE   AUCKLAND
JOHANNESBURG   BLANTYRE   GABORONE
IBADAN   PORTSMOUTH (NH) USA   CHICAGO

Heinemann is a registered trademark of Reed Educational & Professional Publishing Ltd

Text © Jimmy O'Riordan 2002

First published in 2002

06 05 04 03 02
10 9 8 7 6 5 4 3 2 1

British Library Cataloguing in Publication Data
A catalogue record for this book is available from the British Library

ISBN 0 435 55106 X

Typeset by J&L Composition Ltd, Filey, North Yorkshire
Illustrated by Simon Smith
Printed and bound in Great Britain by Scotprint, East Lothian

Websites
Links to appropriate websites are given throughout the book. Although these were up to date at the time of writing, it is essential for teachers to preview these sites before using them with pupils. This will ensure that the URL is still accurate and the content is suitable for your needs. We suggest that you bookmark useful sites and consider enabling pupils to access them through the school intranet. We are bringing this to your attention as we are aware of legitimate sites being appropriated illegally by people wanting to distribute unsuitable or offensive material. We strongly advise you to purchase screening software so that pupils are protected from unsuitable sites and their material.

If you do find that the links given no longer work, or the content is unsuitable, please let us know. Details of changes will be posted on our website.

Cover photograph by: Photodisc

Tel: 01865 888058 www.heinemann.co.uk

Contents

Introduction

This book has been written for students who are studying OCR AS law. I have followed the syllabus exactly so that you can plan your work effectively and know that you have covered what you need for successful examination performance. I have listened carefully to what my own students wanted in terms of a textbook, and clearly some of the books on the market at the moment are just too detailed for their needs. They wanted key points, summaries, jargon guides and exam tips, and they wanted quick revision questions to test their knowledge and boost their confidence. There are no long pages of text in this book, but there is enough detail to allow students to score at the highest level. Everything has been broken into bite-size pieces for easy understanding. I have attempted to make students' lives a bit easier. If you have any comments on the book, whether positive or negative, please let me know. I would be very interested.

Law is constantly changing, so you must keep up to date using the Internet, television and good newspapers. This will give depth to your work and help your understanding. Although I have suggested many web addresses in the text, websites are constantly changing. Before you tackle a Web Activity, ask your teacher to suggest the most appropriate website to make sure that you get the most up-to-date information.

Throughout the book there are references to the use of revision cards. These are simply index cards, obtainable at any good stationers, on which you can put key definitions. These cards can then be carried around by you and used when you have a spare moment. They make your reading and revision process more active and therefore more effective.

Many thanks are due to my wonderful wife Catherine, who looked after our two energetic toddlers Alexander and Elizabeth so that I could get on with writing this book. I would also like to thank all the students, teachers and librarians at High Pavement Sixth Form College for their advice, comments and contributions, particularly Peter Welsby, Laura Burn, Kim Flower, Jane Parker and Kerry Piggott. Lastly, many thanks to Nigel Kelly, Caroline Pratt, Liz Tyler, Susan Kelly, Stephani Havard and Anne Forbes at Heinemann for their excellent support and guidance.

Finally, enjoy your study of law and work your hardest for success.

Jimmy O'Riordan

June 2002

MODULE 1

Machinery of Justice

Civil courts and other methods of dispute resolution

Criminal processes and the criminal courts

Penal system

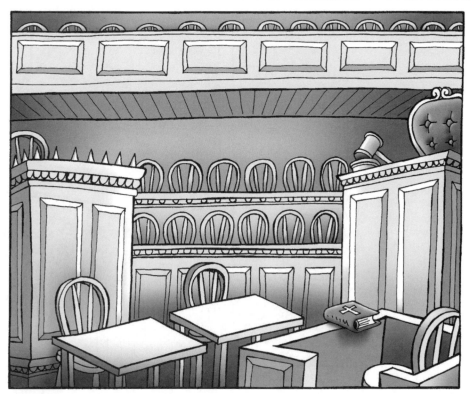

Machinery of justice

UNIT 1

Civil courts

Why do I need to know about the civil courts?

Civil Law involves trying to solve disputes. These disputes may be between individuals, businesses, organizations or public bodies. A full understanding of the civil court system and the areas that connect to it will provide you with a useful insight into your syllabus. Questions on the civil courts will expect you to know about the structure, power and appeal routes available in the civil system. Insight and comments on recent reforms would also be invaluable. The Woolf

Civil disputes

Review of the Civil Court System 1996 is one of the most significant. Also covered in this unit is the tracking system used in the civil courts and information on the work of the County Court and the High Court. This is an important area of your AS course since it has so many links to other parts of your syllabus.

1 The County Court

The County Courts came into existence in 1846 to provide a system of accessible local courts. There are around 220 County Courts in the United Kingdom. The process of using the County Courts is fairly cheap and relatively straightforward. The County Courts deal with a wide range of civil cases.

The County Courts have been a success overall. Most people who have to use them consider the process effective and fair.

Visit activity

County Courts are open to the public and are often attached to the local Crown Court. Try to visit and see both courts in operation. Identify the key differences between the two.

The process used in the civil courts is laid out in the **Civil Procedures Rules 1999**. These rules were an attempt to update court procedures and simplify and update some of the language used in court. The aims of the rules are to:

- ensure both sides are treated fairly, irrespective of their power
- deal with cases according to their importance
- persuade both sides to reveal all relevant facts they hold on the case
- encourage an agreement before or even during a court hearing if possible.

2 Small claims track, fast track and multi-track cases

Pressure exerted by the Consumers' Association led to a new method of dealing with small civil cases. It was felt that the County Court did not represent the interests of claimants who were less well off. People were often discouraged by fears of cost and complexity. To answer these criticisms the **small claims** procedure was created. Recent reforms by Lord Woolf have refined the system further. Cases are sorted into one of three categories called *tracks*. It is hoped that by dealing with cases in this way delays can be avoided and the cases can be heard more quickly.

Web activity

The Consumers' Association is a campaigning pressure group which seeks changes in the law to benefit consumers. Locate their site and identify their current legal campaigns www.consumersassociation.org.

Small claims track, fast track and multi-track

Small claims track

Cases involving sums of money under £5000 are heard in the small claims track. The small claims track is a *method* of conducting a case. The case is heard in an ordinary courtroom in the County Court. Appeals are now allowed from the small claims track since the introduction of the **Human Rights Act 1998**.

The small claims track procedure:

● is less formal than many other court hearings

● involves asking penetrating questions to get to the truth rather than attempting to win by more aggressive methods

● has a limit on total costs, because **claimants** and defendants are encouraged to represent themselves rather than seek professional legal representation

● does not allow the winning side to claim costs

● has a District Judge to hear the case.

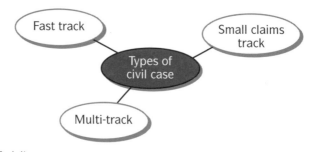

Types of civil cases

Group activity

'**Inquisitorial** processes attempt to get to the truth whilst **adversarial** processes attempt to win.'

These two approaches may produce different evidence and outcomes. Should the following areas of civil court work be adversarial or inquisitorial? Give reasons for your answers.

1 Disputes between people who owe each other money

2 Some divorce cases and custody of children

3 Disputes between landlords and their tenants

4 Settling the financial affairs of people who have died (probate)

5 Personal injury cases

6 Cases relating to the **Race Relations Act 1976**.

Fast track system

This procedure covers cases that involve sums of money between £5000 and £15 000. Both sides of the dispute see information about the case and witnesses before the start of the trial. Fast track cases are normally heard within a day. Costs are capped to reduce the financial burden on the **parties** involved and cases are heard within 30 weeks of being allocated to the fast track.

If fast track cases are particularly complex they may go upwards to the next level, which is called the multi-track system. The vast majority of cases involving the ordinary public are covered by the small claims track and the fast track system.

Multi-track system

These are the most expensive cases heard in the County Court and cover disputes which involve sums of money over £15 000. If cases are particularly complex and time-consuming they may be heard in the multi-track system to allow more time for a solution.

The main changes that have affected the Civil Court system came about through the **Civil Procedure Act 1997**. These are also known as the Woolf Reforms after Lord Woolf. They came into effect in April 1999.

3 The High Court

The High Court also deals with civil cases. Its headquarters are in London and are known as the Royal Courts of Justice. There are also 24 regional High Courts around the country. The High Court deals with more complex cases.

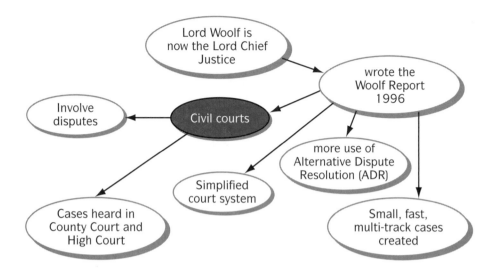

The civil courts

The High Court is divided into three divisions specializing in different types of case.

- The Chancery Division deals with business disputes, companies that become insolvent, and copyright disputes (when one side claims another is stealing its business ideas). The Chancery Division is headed by the Lord Chancellor, although because of his huge workload, the Vice-Chancellor in fact does most of the work. This division has eighteen High Court Judges who hear cases.

- The Queen's Bench Division hears cases involving contract disputes, debt, personal injuries and **tort**. It is the largest of the divisions of the High Court and has 70 High Court Judges headed by the Lord Chief Justice. It is also used for Judicial Review, which happens when judges review decisions taken by public bodies or other large organizations.

- The Family Division was created in 1970. It hears difficult or complex divorce cases and also makes judgments about the custody of children. It is headed by the President and has seventeen judges.

The High Court normally has a single judge hearing cases, but the Queen's Bench Division may have a civil jury in **defamation** cases. In these cases the jury listens to the facts and decides the amount of compensation that is paid to the claimant. Appeals from the High Court are made to the Court of Appeal (Civil Division).

4 Jurisdiction of the courts

Jurisdiction refers to the work of each court or the power of that court to deal with a case. Original jurisdiction refers to where the case was first heard.

Unlike the criminal system, where all cases start in the most junior court, civil cases can start at any point. The civil system is not straightforward. The claimant may have a case involving a relatively small sum of money but extremely complex

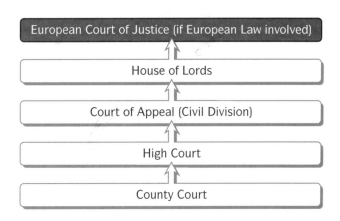

The hierarchy of the civil courts

legal arguments. Another case may involve a great deal of money but a relatively straightforward legal argument. It can be a problem deciding which level of the civil court system to start in.

A number of different courts may claim that it is within their power to hear a case. The Court with the most day to day power is the High Court. Recent reviews, however, mean that County Courts can now hear cases with a much higher monetary value, and this increases the overlap between the various civil courts.

Jurisdiction

Jurisdiction in Magistrates' Courts

Magistrates' jurisdiction on civil matters includes:

- hearing disputes over Council Tax payments
- hearing family cases at the Family Court
- licensing pubs and clubs to sell alcohol
- licensing musical and other entertainment events
- issuing betting and gaming licences.

Jurisdiction in the County Court

The County Court hears a wide range of cases including:

- disputes between people who owe each other money
- uncontested and straightforward divorce cases
- hearings exploring the custody of children
- disputes between landlords and their tenants
- settling the financial affairs of people who have died (probate)
- personal injury cases
- cases involving the **Race Relations Act 1976**.

Jurisdiction in the High Court

The three divisions of the High Court deal with some of the most important and complex civil cases.

- Chancery:
  - copyright disputes covering theft of ideas and inventions
  - claims on trusts, wills and business partnerships
  - bankruptcy proceedings
  - difficult probate cases.
- Queen's Bench Division:
  - contract cases
  - negligence cases
  - personal injury and tort cases.
- Family Division:
  - Divorce cases
  - Child custody cases.

One of the main problems facing the successful claimant in a civil case is collecting the award that they may be given. The Civil Court has no power to order the loser to pay up unless the winner of the case begins another case against them for the outstanding amount.

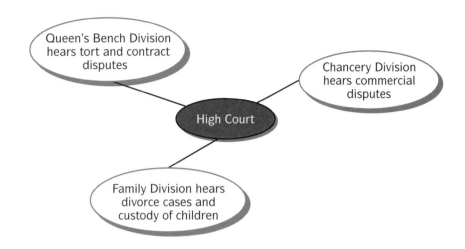

The High Court divisions

This next stage is known as *enforcement proceedings*. It may involve:

- obtaining money directly from the employer of the person who owes the money; this is done by the **Attachment of Earnings Act 1971**

- getting a warrant to take away goods owned by the person; this could involve professionals known as bailiffs

- taking money directly from a bank account or savings account; this is known as a Garnishee Order

- bankruptcy proceedings if the person owes more than £750; this will affect their ability to obtain credit or run a business.

5 Appeals and appellate courts

Appeals

Appeals in the civil court system normally involve moving up to the next most senior judge. There are, however, courts who hear nothing but appeals from other courts. In civil cases there are circumstances where both sides can appeal on either the award made by the court or on the facts of the case and the points of law which arose during the trial.

Appeals from the County Court

The following points will give you an idea of how the appeal process works in the County Court.

- In a small claims track a decision taken by a District Judge would be appealed to a Circuit Judge.

- A fast track case heard by a District Judge would also be appealed to a Circuit Judge.

- A fast track case heard by a Circuit Judge would have an appeal heard by the High Court.
- The most important type of civil case heard in the County Court, the multi-track case, goes for appeal to the Court of Appeal.

Appeals from the High Court

Most decisions from the High Court go to the Court of Appeal (Civil Division) for the appeal hearing.

The High Court also acts as an appeal court. This court is called the Divisional Court. It hears appeals from the courts below it. The Divisional Courts correspond to the three divisions of the High Court (Chancery, Queen's Bench and Family). The most important Divisional Court is the one attached to the Queen's Bench Division that hears Judicial Reviews and applications for **habeas corpus**.

In some rare cases it may be possible to go to the House of Lords for a further appeal. This would normally be on a point of law rather than because of a dispute on the facts of the case.

Appeals need 'leave to appeal', which means permission. This is only given when there is a genuine chance of a successful outcome or there are other strong reasons for allowing an appeal to proceed.

The appeals system

Legal case: *Tanfern Ltd v Cameron-MacDonald (2000)*

In *Tanfern Ltd v Cameron-MacDonald (2000)* the Court of Appeal (Civil Division) explained that second appeals would become something of a rarity. The Government was keen to see this happen to reduce the considerable pressure on the civil court process. It was feared that the introduction of the **Human Rights Act 1998** would open a floodgate of claims and appeals.

It was therefore felt that:

● only appeals with a real prospect of success should be allowed

● only one appeal for a civil case should be allowed unless there were very exceptional circumstances

● the automatic right to appeal should be withdrawn and permission would be needed in almost all appeals to the Court of Appeal.

The predicted surge in demand for appeals generated by the **Human Rights Act 1998** has not happened to any great degree. The changes remain in force, however, and most regard them as a 'qualified success'.

Tanfern Ltd vs Cameron-MacDonald (2000) has led to fewer appeals

6 Problems of using the courts

Problems of cost, delay and complexity still deter many citizens with a legal issue from using the civil courts system.

Cost

Changes brought about by the **Access to Justice Act 1999** have made justice more achievable for some, but have possibly reduced access for others. Conditional fee arrangements (also known as 'no win no fee') have allowed many more people to access the civil court system, but problems remain for those clients with weaker cases and with solicitors who attempt to increase their share of the 'winnings' from successfully completed cases. Some lawyers are increasingly seeing the civil case as a ready source of income and are quite happy to encourage litigation to 'solve' the dispute.

Delay

Significant delay was present in both County Court and High Court cases, although it is now getting a little better. Three years in the County Court and up to five years in the High Court between the incident and the trial were common. One result of this has been less effective trials, since witnesses are hazy on events that happened so long ago, possibly under circumstances of panic and emergency.

The delay issue affects the financial and psychological status of some parties more than others, of course. Businesses, local authorities or health trusts have no emotional involvement with the case. A sick or elderly claimant who is possibly using the civil system for the first time may feel differently. They may well suffer sleepless nights worrying about the cost and whether they were right to pursue the case, given the impact on their nerves and health.

Complexity

Legislation generated from UK and European sources may increase the complexity of civil cases. Legal representation then sometimes becomes essential, pushing up costs for both sides.

Out-of-court settlements

As a result of the problems of cost, delay and complexity, many ordinary claimants may accept woefully inadequate out-of-court settlements from the defendants. This is particularly true if the defendants are large companies or public bodies who have the resources to string the case out.

Lord Woolf's Review

The problems of using the civil courts have been reduced to a certain extent by the Woolf Review proposals. Encouragement to use the many alternatives to the formal court process and a less adversarial approach have improved the process.

Revision checklist

1 The County Courts are local courts designed to hear civil cases involving unpaid bills, personal injury cases and uncontested divorce cases.

2 Small claims track deals with cases involving sums of money less than £5000.

3 Fast track deals with sums of money between £5000 and £15000.

4 Multi-track deals with cases involving sums of money greater than £15000 or more complex cases.

5 The High Court deals with more important civil cases.

6 The High Court is split into three divisions which have a corresponding Divisional Court for appeals attached: Chancery Division, Queen's Bench Division and Family Division.

7 Jurisdiction of the courts refers to their power to hear a case. Overlapping powers make the civil court structure complex.

8 Appeals in the civil court system are normally to the next judge up: District Judges to Circuit Judges; Circuit Judges to High Court judges.

9 Problems of using the civil court system include: cost, delay, complexity and out-of-court settlements.

10 Major reforms of the civil courts have occurred as a result of the Woolf Review 1996 and **Civil Procedure Act 1997**. Many of the reforms actually came into force in April 1999.

Quick revision questions

1 What are the chief functions of the County Court?

2 What types of cases are heard as *small claims, fast* and *multi-track?*

3 What is the work of the three divisions of the High Court?

4 Where would a dispute involving £4500 of building work be heard?

5 What court would deal with a personal injury case worth £250 000?

6 Where would an uncontested divorce case involving children be heard?

7 What does *jurisdiction* mean?

8 What is the main appeal principle in civil cases?

9 What are the main problems that users encounter when using the courts?

10 Outline the key reforms brought about by the Woolf Review.

Exam question

1 a What are the main problems facing a claimant who wishes to take a case to the civil court? [20 marks]

b How could an individual access the civil court system more effectively? [25 marks]

Exam answer guide

1 a Problems facing the claimant could include:
- ✓ costs such as legal fees, time off work to attend hearings and other expenses that could be involved in such an undertaking
- ✓ costs of the other side if you lose a fast track or multi-track case
- ✓ delay to the case, perhaps for several weeks or months
- ✓ complexity of the system that intimidates ordinary citizens
- ✓ the other side may be much more powerful, i.e. a business or local authority.

Mention as many as points as you can think of, but focus on a limited number and develop some more in-depth points.

b Possible solutions might include:
- ✓ use of conditional fee arrangements or 'no win no fee'
- ✓ use of an advice agency or trade union for support
- ✓ sorting out the problem before the court hearing
- ✓ use a trade association, watchdog or media source for help
- ✓ consider application for Community Legal Service funding.

The answer would benefit from *your view*, so after you have considered the issue make sure you give an opinion on access to justice.

UNIT 2

Alternatives to the courts

Key points

1 Arbitration
2 Conciliation
3 Mediation
4 Role and composition of administrative tribunals

Why do I need to know about alternatives to courts?

Questions set on alternatives to courts are popular since this area is now seen as an important part of the Government's solution to pressures on the civil courts system. You need to understand the background to the recent reforms, the key alternatives suggested and how effective they are. The Legatt Report has reviewed the tribunal system and suggested improvements. Read section 6 of Unit 1 to refresh your memory on the problems faced by users of the civil court system.

Alternative dispute resolution – courts can be expensive!

1 Arbitration

The court system is under strain in a way unseen before in its long history. People are resorting to the courts more often. The enormous rise in consumption of goods, more complex working patterns and greater confidence have increased the scope for disputes. Employees, consumers, patients and even students are resorting to the courts to get 'justice'. The result has been enormous pressure on the courts. The Woolf reforms of the civil court system have attempted to reduce the burden on the courts and encourage a different approach to dispute solving.

Arbitration is one method to resolve disputes without court action. Both sides to the argument voluntarily agree to an independent third party making a decision on their case. The process in governed by the **Arbitration Act 1996**. The details of the case and the process are normally put into writing to keep everything clear. Arbitration is the most formal of the methods we will consider in this unit.

The arbitration style can however vary considerably depending on the parties involved and their needs. There may be a need for something very informal or, at the other extreme, a process which does not look unlike a formal court. The courts can enforce awards made by the arbitrator, although, as in some formal civil cases, the claimant may in the end see little if any of the money promised.

Web activity

Find the site for the Institute of Arbitrators at www.instituteofarbitrators.org. What are the key functions of their organization?

Arbitration can be cheaper than courts

Industrial arbitration

One of the best known organizations working in this area is the Arbitration and Conciliation Advisory Service (ACAS). ACAS is Government-funded. It often finds itself arbitrating between trade unions and employers in industrial disputes. ACAS has a record of being respected by both sides for its impartiality and effectiveness.

Consumer arbitration

Many organizations involved in the commercial world have introduced arbitration schemes to help relationships between consumers and businesses. The building industry has the Federation of Master Builders (FMB) and the travel industry has the Association of British Travel Agents (ABTA).

Web activity

Check out the websites of ACAS, FMB and ABTA. What services do they offer if there is a dispute?

Commercial arbitration

The complexity of business contracts makes disputes likely. One way to limit the damage and expense caused by such disagreements is to have a safety valve built into any agreements. The two parties will seek arbitration if they cannot quickly solve a problem that arises between them. The *Scott v Avery (1855)* case signalled this new approach, so a clause in a contract pre-agreeing arbitration is called a Scott Avery Clause.

Strengths of the arbitration system

- There is a knowledgeable arbitrator who may have heard hundreds of similar cases.
- The facts of the arbitrated case are not public information, so companies and individuals who value privacy may prefer this style.
- Claimants and defendants can choose the best time and place for them.
- Arbitration is normally quicker and cheaper than formal court procedures.

Weaknesses of the arbitration system

- There is no public airing of the wrong done, which some claimants want.
- There may be difficulties when the case covers technical legal points outside the capabilities of the participants.
- Awards can be challenged by either party when they believe serious irregularities have taken place.
- Individuals may still be much weaker if an organization is defending a case and seeks prior professional guidance.

2 Conciliation

Conciliation involves a neutral third party attempting to help solve a dispute. The conciliator raises relevant issues and actively suggests appropriate solutions. There are a number of official bodies which offer such support, including the Centre for Dispute Resolution. The service is quick and cheap, although the claimant and defendant are not bound by the process and can break off at any point if they choose. More formal and costlier processes may then of course have to be considered.

3 Mediation

Mediation involves an independent third party attempting to find some common ground between two parties in dispute. The mediator acts as a message carrier between the two. The process will only work if there really is some midway point that the two actively make attempts to find acceptable. One well known organization offering a mediation service is Relate. It will, for example, help any couple seeking to avoid a divorce.

Ombudsmen

An ombudsman is an independent third party who tries to solve disputes concerning poor service offered by public services. There is an ombudsman who deals with tax issues, and others for the National Health Service and for local Government. The **Court and Legal Services Act 1990** introduced an ombudsman to deal with legal services and conveyancing (buying and selling houses).

Mediation

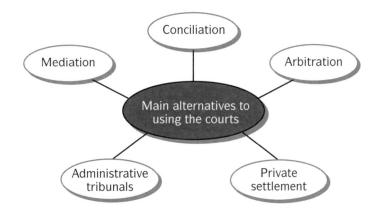

Main alternatives to the courts

4 Role and composition of administrative tribunals

The Government sets up administrative tribunals. Their main function is to enforce citizens' rights to welfare and other social security entitlements. They have a wide jurisdiction covering 75 different areas of life, with more than 2000 panels sitting to hear cases around the country. All decisions made by administrative tribunals can be judicially reviewed.

Some tribunals, such as the Social Security and National Insurance Tribunals, operate as a nationwide network, while others are proud of their independence.

Examples of administrative tribunals include:

● Social Security Appeals Tribunal

● Immigration Appeals Tribunal

● Mental Health Review Tribunal

● Rent tribunals

● Employment tribunals.

The Legatt Report reviewed the present system of tribunals in August 2001. It revealed that the 70 tribunals dealt with over a million cases per year. The Social Security Tribunal was the largest, hearing 270 000 appeals in one year. The Legatt Report recommended the following changes:

● better access to information and service

● a Customer Charter setting down standards to be reached

● improved tribunal procedures

● more use of information technology.

┌─ **Web activity** ──┐
│ For the background to the Legatt Review of the tribunal system see │
│ www.tribunals-review.org.uk.   │
└──┘

The development of the tribunal system is a little bit like the development of the courts system in general. It has responded to changes over a period of time, and now it looks to the outsider very chaotic and unstructured.

These key features apply to most tribunals.

- The tribunal is set up as a panel of three individuals, one of whom is normally qualified or experienced in the area the tribunal covers.

- The other two are lay members who are expected to have some knowledge of the tribunal's remit.

- The chairman is appointed by the Lord Chancellor's Department, and is therefore to a certain extent distanced from outside pressures.

- The process in often less formal than a court hearing.

- Apart from Employment Tribunals, **precedent** does not have to be followed.

- Decisions are not always supported by full explanations, which makes appeals difficult.

Strengths of the tribunal system

- Cases are normally dealt with more quickly and more cheaply than through the courts.

- Each tribunal has an expert. In many ways this is an advantage over a court, which has to call in outside witnesses for specialist opinion.

- Procedure is more informal, which helps clients who are unfamiliar with putting their case in a public setting.

- The cases are heard in private, which can benefit business confidentiality and also help people with delicate issues to discuss.

Weaknesses of the tribunal system

- Power imbalance often exists with an individual versus a large business or Government department.

- No explanations for decisions taken make meaningful appeals unlikely.

- Tax and social security legislation and procedures are so complex that clients without expert support are often at a disadvantage.

- No funding for cases disadvantages individual claimants or defendants.

Exam tip

Revision classes are some of the most important classes of your course. Be particularly attentive.

Revision checklist

1 Arbitration allows an independent third party to make decisions on a dispute if both parties agree.

2 It is possible to have industrial, consumer and commercial arbitration.

3 Strengths of arbitration include: knowledgeable arbitrator, privacy, cheaper and more convenient than courts.

4 Weaknesses of arbitration include: no publicity, technicalities may cause problems, awards can be challenged, and individuals are at a disadvantage if faced with large companies or public organizations.

5 Conciliation involves taking an active approach to solving disputes.

6 Mediation involves trying to find common ground between two parties.

7 Ombudsmen investigate public bodies and their poor administration.

8 Administrative tribunals cover areas such as: social security, immigration, mental health, rent, and employment.

9 Strengths of administrative tribunals include: speed, experts, informality and privacy.

10 Weaknesses of administrative tribunals include: power imbalance, no explanations for decisions, cases can be complex so individuals are disadvantaged, and no legal funding for individuals.

Quick revision questions

1 What are the key elements to arbitration?

2 What types of arbitration are available?

3 Name three strengths of arbitration.

4 Name three weaknesses of arbitration.

5 What is the difference between *conciliation* and *mediation*?

6 What does an ombudsman do?

7 Name some key areas that administrative tribunals work in.

8 What report has recently reviewed the tribunal system?

9 What knowledge is expected of the members of a tribunal?

10 Name the key pros and cons of the tribunal system.

1 a What are the main ways parties with civil disputes can resolve their differences? [25 marks]

b Why have arbitration methods that avoid court hearings increased in recent years? [20 marks]

Exam answer guide

1 a Include the following points:
- ✓ negotiation
- ✓ mediation
- ✓ conciliation
- ✓ arbitration
- ✓ tribunals
- ✓ courts.

Show some in-depth analysis by choosing one or two points to explore in more detail. *Give your opinion.* Do you think this is a better approach than using the courts?

b Include the following points:
- ✓ legal costs have increased
- ✓ court delays and complexity
- ✓ effectiveness of tribunals
- ✓ busy lives – no time for formal hearings
- ✓ encouragement by the Government
- ✓ more information about alternatives available.

Do not go into too much detail, given the number of marks and what the question has asked. A brief outline is all that is needed.

UNIT 3

European Court of Justice

Key points

1 The European Court of Justice (ECJ)
2 Article 234 referrals
3 Relationship of ECJ to English courts

Why do I need to know about the European Court of Justice?

Questions on European law will presume students understand the key institutions and processes of the European legal system. Questions often ask about the relationship between English law and European law. Which one is 'supreme'? Which one takes priority? Article 234 sounds a bit more difficult than it is and simply involves a process of referring a relevant legal matter involving European Law to the European Court of Justice. Your understanding of the English legal system will assist you in coming to terms with the European system of law.

ECJ

1 The European Court of Justice (ECJ)

The European Union is one of the most powerful organizations in the world and was first set up as a legal organization. As a result it has its own legal system and its own courts. The key court of the European Union is the European Court of Justice (ECJ).

Unfortunately the ECJ is often confused with another important court in Europe called the European Court of Human Rights. This is an entirely separate court. The European Court of Justice is not the same as the European Court on Human Rights. The European Court of Human Rights focuses on human rights issues entirely and sits in Strasbourg. It is concerned solely with the European Convention of Human Rights.

The European Court of Justice has two main aims which are outlined in the **Treaty of Rome (1957)**. The first is the efficient interpretation of European law. The second is the fair and effective application of that European law.

English courts may come across legislation which has a European dimension. The English court will attempt to interpret and apply it as if it were English law. In some circumstances points of law will arise which need clarification. English law may end up in the House of Lords but European law must go to the ECJ to ensure all member states use the law consistently. This process of referring cases to the ECJ uses Article 234 (see section 2 on referrals). It is compulsory if the case has gone to the highest court in the member country.

European Court of Justice functions include:

- taking action against member states who do not comply with their EU obligations. The action is normally taken brought by the Commission but sometimes by another member state. The Court may fine the member state if they are found guilty

- disciplining institutions of the European Union if they do not meet their responsibilities. It may 'penalize silence or inaction'

- interpreting European Union law when member states run into difficulties with the meaning and intentions of the legislation

- annulling legislation if it is not suitable for the overall aims of the ECJ or the EU. A member state, the Council, the Commission and sometimes the Parliament may apply for annulment of Community legislation

- hearing actions for damages against Community institutions and making rulings on liability and amounts for compensation.

Composition of the European Court of Justice

The European Court of Justice consists of fifteen judges, one from each member state of the EU. The fifteen judges do not act in the interests of their own countries, but in the interests of the whole European Union. They must be completely impartial since decisions may sometimes be made which are not in the immediate interests of their home country but will in the long run benefit all or the majority of member countries.

Glossary

The **Treaty of Rome** was the agreement that started the development of the European Union in 1957. The United Kingdom did not join until 1973. The Treaty is law in all fifteen European Union countries.

Eight other legal experts called Advocates General advise the judges. They research the cases, supply analysis of the issues and attempt to provide possible solutions to the legal problem. This is intended to assist the judges in their legal discussions and rulings.

Workings of the European Court of Justice

The ECJ has a different way of dealing with the law than we are used to. Most of the process is carried out in writing, and there is little formal courtroom activity.

The Advocates General present independent legal views. When the judges have made a decision on the case, the result is always given in writing and no information is given on who disagreed with the decision.

The ECJ differs in one other crucial way. Precedent, which means following previous decisions on similar cases, does not apply to them. This gives them greater flexibility on each case heard, as they are not bound by the outcomes of others previously heard.

Group activity

Get hold of *The Times* newspaper and look at law reports which involve the Law Lords. Three Law Lords normally sit together and give their views, which are then published in full. They sometimes disagree with each other and give reasons for their opposition. Judgments of the ECJ are also published, but only the majority view is put forward.

1 Why do you think the ECJ judges prefer to remain anonymous in their decision-making?

2 What are the pros and cons of such a system?

The evolving legal work of the European Union forced the creation in 1989 of another court to take some of the pressure off the ECJ. This court is known as the Court of First Instance. It hears many cases which require long examination of the facts. This leaves the ECJ free to concentrate on more important issues. Some of these will be examined in the next section.

Glossary

Interdependency means countries coming together to share responsibilities for important economic and legal projects. In the end they come to depend upon one another.

2 Article 234 referrals

The European Union (EU) consists of fifteen countries with different legal, political, cultural and social perspectives. The law of the European Union provides an opportunity to bring these diverse members together. Later in this unit we will look at which legal system takes priority, or even if this has any real meaning given the **interdependency** of the members and their affairs.

One way of ensuring standardization of the EU legal system is to refer any law that has some uncertainty about it to one authority for a verdict. This authority is the European Court of Justice.

Article 234 referrals ensure that the ECJ has an opportunity to give its interpretation on any EU law that needs clarification.

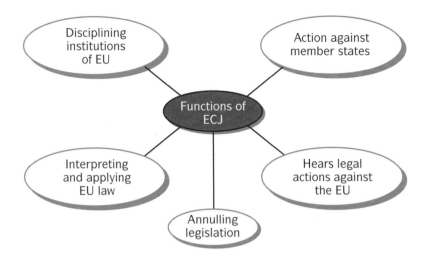

Functions of the European Court of Justice

Legal Case: *Levi v Tesco (2001)*

The recent case of *Levi v Tesco (2001)* illustrates the power of the ECJ. Tesco had been selling cut-price Levi jeans. Levi was keen to see this stop and took the supermarket to court on a brand-name issue. The European Court of Justice ruled in favour of Levi and ordered Tesco to stop selling the 'quality' jeans at reduced prices.

Cheap jeans – ECJ acts

3 Relationship of ECJ to English courts

The people of the United Kingdom elect a Government which passes legislation in the form of Acts of Parliament. The English court system interprets and applies this law. Since 1 January 1973, however, we have been a member of another legal and political system, the European Union. The courts now have the function of interpreting and applying European law as well. The problem of a clash is therefore possible. Which system should take priority? Which one should be supreme?

We must look at what might happen if each member state could choose to obey or not obey as it liked. What would be the result? Since the whole basis of the EU is designed to bring about closer economic, social and political ties, all member states 'doing their own thing' would mean the end of the European Union.

The United Kingdom voluntarily signed the **European Communities Act 1972** (which made the UK a member of the EU effective from 1 January 1973) after a **referendum** of the population and has therefore agreed to the supremacy of the European Union's legal system. If there is a conflict between the two, European law takes priority over English law.

On the other hand, the United Kingdom Government has the option of disobeying the supremacy of European law, but this would mean leaving the European Union.

Revision checklist

1 The European Court of Justice is the court of the European Union and deals with the interpretation and application of European Union law.

2 The ECJ can take action against member states and institutions of the EU.

3 The ECJ consists of fifteen judges, one from each member state, supported by eight Advocates General.

4 The ECJ has little formal courtroom activity. Judgments come in writing.

5 Rulings of the ECJ do not indicate if there was disagreement within the court over the issue.

6 The Court of First Instance was created to help with the work of the ECJ.

7 Article 234 deals with referring cases to the ECJ for clarification.

8 The UK came into the EU in 1973 when it signed the **European Communities Act of 1972**.

9 The ECJ takes priority over English courts.

10 Ignoring the jurisdiction of the ECJ would only be possible if the UK left the EU.

1 What is the difference between the ECJ and the European Court of Human Rights?

2 What are the key objectives of the ECJ?

3 What powers has the ECJ against EU member states?

4 How many judges sit on the ECJ?

5 What does an Advocate General do?

6 Why was the Court of First Instance created?

7 What is the purpose of Article 234?

8 When did the UK sign the **European Communities Act**?

9 Does English or European law take priority when there is a conflict?

10 Is there any way of avoiding EU legislation?

Exam question

1 a Outline the key functions of the European Court of Justice. [20 marks]

b Why is European law so important? [25 marks]

Exam answer guide

1 a The key functions of the ECJ are:
✓ taking action against member states
✓ disciplining institutions of the EU
✓ interpreting EU law
✓ annulling weak EU law
✓ awarding damages against EU institutions if necessary.

b EU law is important because:
✓ it provides a legal rather than a military settlement for disputes
✓ it underpins the economic life of the EU
✓ it allows EU citizens protection throughout the EU
✓ it supports the setting up of businesses and other organizations
✓ it provides an independent voice in a diverse European organization.

The question prompts you to give a rather one-sided view, which is the positive view of EU law. Many people, of course, find some legislation from the EU burdensome. Mention the negatives, but *stick closely to the question's main thrust on this occasion.*

UNIT 4

Police powers

Key points

1 Powers to stop and search
2 Powers of arrest
3 Powers of detention
4 Treatment of suspects at the police station
5 Balance between individual rights and need for investigative powers

Why do I need to know about police powers?

Examination questions on the police present an opportunity to explore complex questions about rights and responsibilities. On the one hand is our need for protection and investigation of crime, and on the other our desire for privacy and freedom. To answer questions effectively you need to know the law on police powers. Of particular importance is the **Police and Criminal Evidence Act 1984**. This is the key piece of legislation that aims to balance the powers of the police with our protection as citizens. Another area of importance is the **Human Rights Act 1999**. To answer questions effectively, look at the issues from all sides, that is, the police, the victim and the suspect.

Police power – defendants' rights

1 Powers to stop and search

The police have powers to stop and search members of the public if they suspect they have stolen items in their possession or hold offensive weapons. Suspicion must not be based on any of the following factors:

- colour of skin
- racial group
- previous criminal record
- personal dress code
- other stereotyping.

The **Police and Criminal Evidence Act 1984**, also known as PACE, gives police these powers to stop and search. In addition, the **Misuse of Drugs Act 1971** gives police the power to stop and search if they have reasonable belief that they are likely to find illegal drugs.

Glossary

Presumption of innocence means that someone is assumed to be innocent until they are proved guilty by a criminal court.

Stop and search has been a necessary but controversial area of police powers for some time. Some communities feel that powers to stop and search have at times been misused by the police. Some figures from the Home Office show a disproportionate percentage of young black men have been stopped and searched compared to their profile in the population. The Metropolitan Police Authority (which covers London) has come in for the most scrutiny in this area. **Presumption of innocence** is the bedrock of the English legal system, so the stop-and-search tool seems unfair and irritating to many people.

There are some safeguards built into PACE to give protection to potential suspects. These include:

- The suspect has the right to see identification if the police officer is in plain clothes.
- The police officer must state his/her name, police station and the reason for the search (Section 2 PACE 1984).
- A written record of the search must be made (Section 3 PACE 1984).

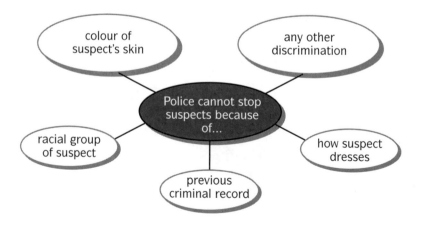

Factors that must not cause suspicion

Legal case: *Osman v DPP (1999)*

Osman v DPP (1999) underlined the need for police to state name, police station and reasons for arrest. If not, the search is illegal.

2 Powers of arrest

Section 24 of the **Police and Criminal Evidence Act 1984** (PACE) outlines the powers police possess to arrest individuals. An arrest normally involves a person being taken by the police to a police station and kept there for questioning. The reason for arrest must be stated; this will normally be suspicion that they have committed a crime.

Magistrates can issue a warrant for arrest if a defendant fails to attend court or if the police apply for a warrant to arrest a suspect. Police may also arrest if there is a breach of the peace or using provisions given to them by PACE.

If a person is arrested it must be for an 'arrestable offence', according to section 24 of PACE. This will include:

● any offence which has a fixed sentence of imprisonment (murder)

● any offence which could carry a sentence of five years (robbery)

● any offence which Parliament says should be an arrestable offence.

If the police are faced with a defendant who has not committed an arrestable offence but they think some offence has been committed, they can arrest in the following circumstances:

● if they cannot verify the person's name or address

● if an arrest would protect the individual or others, or property

● if an arrest would protect someone who was defenceless, such as a child or an elderly person.

The police officer must have 'reasonable grounds' to believe an offence has been committed. This is called the *objective test*. Would an ordinary person think it was reasonable that the officer arrested the suspect? For example, it is prohibited for the police to stop drivers randomly during the evening to see whether they have been drinking too much. They must have some reasonable suspicion of drunk driving. The driver might be driving very slowly or very quickly, or going through a red light; this might be reasonable grounds for suspicion.

There are two other areas which give police power to arrest.

● Arrest for a 'breach of the peace', an old common law, allows a great deal of flexibility for police to take someone into custody. 'Breach of the peace' is the causing of harm or the fear that harm may take place. It was retained in section 26 of PACE 1984.

● The **Public Order Act 1986** allows sweeping powers for the police to make arrests at public demonstrations and elsewhere. The Act was very controversial when first passed, with many people questioning its denial of civil liberties.

Exam tip

Try to remember the precise sections of PACE that are relevant. These details will show your command of this topic.

When the suspect has been arrested, the police officer must make it clear to the suspect why they have been arrested (Section 28 PACE 1984) and then take them to a police station as soon as possible (Section 30 PACE 1984). Other protection includes:

- The reading of a caution to the suspect. This is a warning that what is said *and not said* may be given in evidence against them. The caution is normally given at the time of the arrest, but if not, it must be read before questioning of the suspect begins.

- Entitlement to a tape-recording of the interview: this must always take place (Section 60 PACE 1984).

- Right to let someone know that they have been arrested: this might be a solicitor or a member of their family (Section 56 PACE 1984). This can be suspended if the police believe they may tip off other members of a gang. Delay can be no more than 36 hours.

- Right to a private consultation with their solicitor (Section 58 PACE 1984): this could include a duty solicitor who is provided free of charge at the station.

- Suspects who are vulnerable, such as children or people with a mental impairment, must have a suitable adult present when the police question them. The suitable adult could be a parent/guardian or a social worker.

Police and Criminal Evidence Act

Citizen's arrest

A citizen's arrest happens when an ordinary person detains a suspect. This is very risky for the person arresting the suspect. If the offence is not an arrestable offence, then the person detaining a suspect may be left open to criminal proceedings themselves. Section 24 of PACE 1984 gives grounds for citizen's arrest when:

● an arrestable offence is under way or it is reasonably believed that such an offence is about to be committed

● an arrestable offence has been committed and there are reasonable grounds for suspicion.

3 Powers of detention

Section 41 of PACE states that, under normal circumstances, a person must be released within 24 hours of arrest unless they are formally charged with an offence. Sections 42 and 43 of PACE 1984 allow further extensions, but the maximum is 96 hours in detention without charge.

If the offence is a serious arrestable offence, the extension to the basic 24 hours without charge must be made by a senior police officer, i.e. a superintendent or above. The next period of detention must be authorized by a magistrate and cannot exceed the 96 hours total without charge (Section 44 PACE 1984).

4 Treatment of suspects at the police station

The custody officer is responsible for seeing that the provisions of PACE are observed while the suspect is held in custody. A record must be kept of:

● the suspect's name, address and other personal details

● time of arrest and arrival at police station

● possessions of the suspect when arrested

● possessions which are confiscated by the custody officer

● details of any search of the suspect

● fingerprint information.

The custody officer is ultimately responsible for the correct procedures being carried out at the police station and the safety and well-being of the suspect. One area related to this is the provision of food, suitable breaks between questioning, and sleep for the detained suspect. The suspect should not be questioned for more than two hours without a break, and there should be provision for eight hours' sleep every 24 hours for the suspect. The last responsibilities are covered under Code C of PACE 1984.

Searches and samples at the police station

Section 54 PACE allows non-intimate searches of the suspect. The code of practice allows strip searches, where the suspect removes more than the outer layering of clothing. These searches must be in private and must be sensitive.

An intimate search is allowed, provided the permission of a superintendent or above is given. These searches involve all orifices other than the mouth. The officer giving permission for such searches must believe that there could be class A drugs hidden, or items which would cause harm to the suspect. In normal circumstances a nurse or doctor should carry out the search, but in an emergency a police officer may have to perform the task.

Samples of blood, urine, swabs from orifices other than mouth, or pubic hair are allowed under section 62 of PACE. The samples can only be taken by a nurse or a doctor. Section 117 allows reasonable force to be used if the suspect refuses permission for searches or for samples to be taken.

PACE ensure rest and food for suspects

5 Balance between individual rights and need for investigative powers

Clearly a lawful and regulated society benefits the vast majority of citizens. We expect law and order, but we are often irritated when the work of investigating authorities causes us inconvenience. There has to be a balance between our rights and the expectations we have of the police to apprehend, detain and deliver suspects to our courts.

The Police and Criminal Evidence Act 1984

This is now the key piece of legislation that not only lays out the authority of the police, but also their responsibilities to ordinary citizens. The powers include the right to stop and search individuals, to take fingerprints, to collect samples such as saliva and hair and to search homes and cars. To many people, these actions may be seen as very disturbing. To protect the freedom of suspects, important rights were built into the legislation. They give directions on what the suspect should expect whilst detained. They include the right to:

- a telephone call
- a private conversation with a solicitor
- regular breaks
- food and water.

Without these safeguards, the suspect would be in a vulnerable position and the police in a very powerful one. The guidance is known as the Code of Practice. It is not legally binding on the police, but is an influential protector of rights nevertheless.

The Human Rights Act 1998

The **Human Rights Act 1998** attempts to provide a balance by stating some of our basic rights. Article 5 is particularly relevant here:

'Everyone has the right to liberty and security. No one shall be deprived of his liberty except in the following circumstances . . .'

The 'following circumstances' include the arrest of people who have committed or are about to commit an offence. It is then a balancing act between our right to liberty and our need to feel secure.

Group activity

- Four men are seen driving in a car at 3am.
- Do the police have the right to stop, search and question?
- Do the men have the right to drive a car at night?
- Should they expect to be stopped?
- Do they deserve to be stopped?

Revision checklist

1 Section 1 PACE (1984) gives the police rights to search individuals and vehicles.

2 The suspect is entitled to the officer's name, police station and reason for the search. If not, the search is unlawful *(Osman v DPP (1999))*.

3 Section 24 PACE gives police the power to arrest for an arrestable offence. This is one that has a fixed sentence, at least a five-year sentence, or is arrestable according to Parliament.

4 An arrest can also take place if the officer cannot verify the name and address of the suspect, if arrest would protect others, or if the arrest would protect a defenceless person.

5 A breach of the peace can be used as grounds for arrest (Section 24 PACE), as can offences under the **Public Order Act 1986**.

6 The officer must have reasonable grounds for arrest. This is the objective test. What would a reasonable person believe?

7 The suspect is protected by a range of points in PACE: the right to a solicitor, the right to breaks and sleep, and the right to release within 24–96 hours if not charged.

8 The custody officer is responsible for the treatment of the suspect whilst at the police station. Terms of PACE must be observed at all times.

9 Intimate searches can be made and samples of blood and other material taken from the suspect. There are strict rules for these actions under PACE.

10 The **Human Rights Act 1999** specifically mentions arrests under Article 5, although there is an acknowledged right for the police to arrest suspects lawfully.

Quick revision questions

1 What must police not take into consideration when stopping someone to search them?

2 What is the key piece of legislation giving power to stop and search?

3 What safeguards do members of the public have when being stopped by the police?

4 What is an *arrestable offence*?

5 What is *breach of the peace*?

6 What rights has the suspect once in the police station?

7 Why is a citizen's arrest a risky thing to do?

8 What rights have the police got to search and take samples from suspects?

9 What is a *Code of Practice*?

10 How does the **Human Rights Act 1998** affect police behaviour?

1 a What are the main safeguards given to suspects arrested for alleged offences? [20 marks]

b Do you think they favour the police or the offender? [25 marks]

Exam answer guide

The Police and Criminal Evidence Act and its Codes give the following safeguards:

- ✓ right to identification from the police and to know the reasons for arrest
- ✓ right to a solicitor in private
- ✓ right to release within 24–96 hours if not charged
- ✓ right to breaks, food and sleep when being questioned
- ✓ right to see the Codes of Practice police have to obey.

The police have the right to

- ✓ arrest the suspect
- ✓ take them to the police station against their will
- ✓ question them for up to 96 hours with permission from magistrates
- ✓ take blood samples and other bodily fluids
- ✓ search their houses and cars.

When answering part **b**, you should compare these police powers with the answers given in part **a**. On the whole, both seem to have powers and protections. For one, however, it is routine daily work and for the other it may be a frightening and new experience. The rules are well intentioned, but they may rely to a certain extent on the people applying them in the police station and the personality and confidence of the suspect.

Criminal courts

Key points

1 Pre-trial matters
2 Bail
3 Mode of trial
4 Committal proceedings
5 Jurisdictions of Magistrates', Youth and Crown Courts
6 Appeals
7 The role of the Criminal Cases Review Commission

Why do I need to know about the criminal courts?

Examination questions will expect you to know the functions and workings of the two main criminal courts, the Magistrates' Court and the Crown Court. The criminal courts hear some of the most serious criminal offences. You need to understand the appeal process and the reasons for the creation of and the role of the Criminal Cases Review Commission. The Auld Report will have a major impact on the workings of the criminal court system. You need to be aware of the proposals and the effects of the Auld Report.

Justice

1 Pre-trial matters

There are many stages between an offence and a criminal trial. The police play their part investigating, the Crown Prosecution Service (CPS) considers whether the trial should go ahead or not, and then the courts themselves have to go through their own pre-trial procedures. These processes are designed to reduce costly trial proceedings and prevent people who should not be in front of a court from appearing there. The overall structure is known as the **Criminal Justice System** (CJS).

Role of the police

The police have an *investigative role* when an offence is committed. They collect evidence from the scene of the crime, interview witnesses, arrest and question the suspect, and charge them if they feel they have sufficient evidence. Many people who are charged are later found innocent. The charge allows the police more time to conduct their investigations and indicates to the accused the direction of the case and the possible need for legal advice.

Minor offences are often dealt with by a *caution*. A caution is a warning to the offender to mend their ways. A record is kept of cautions given by the police. A caution can only be given, however, if the offender admits to being guilty and is prepared to accept the caution in good faith. Most cases of drunk and disorderly are dealt with by cautions when the offender sobers up, normally the next morning. Cautions are now also going to be the norm for the possession of cannabis, rather than a court appearance before the Magistrates.

Cautions are particularly effective with children. The **Crime and Disorder Act 1998** has a number of provisions affecting young people. It strengthened the cautionary element (now called *warning and reprimand*) with regard to children in the hope of keeping them out of court and out of the Criminal Justice System completely.

The Crown Prosecution Service

The Crown Prosecution Service (CPS) was created from the **Prosecution of Offences Act 1985**. Once the police have gathered evidence on the offence, the case is passed to the CPS, which has to make the decision on whether to proceed with the case or drop it. Its main function is to prosecute offenders on behalf of the state, but it will only prosecute a case if there is enough evidence and prosecution is in the public interest.

The CPS has come in for criticism for dropping too many cases before they come to trial. This criticism came from victims and their families, and also from two reviews into the work of the CPS, the Narey Review 1997 and the Glidewell Report 1998. As a result of these pressures the Crown Prosecution Service was restructured and now has 42 regional centres rather than one central office. It also has more liaison with local police forces. It was hoped that users would find the CPS more accessible and more understanding.

The main functions of the CPS are:

● reviewing evidence to assess the chance of successful prosecution
● giving guidance on the evidence that is submitted by the police
● prosecuting cases in the Magistrates' Courts
● hiring (known as instructing) qualified advocates to prosecute cases in the Crown Court.

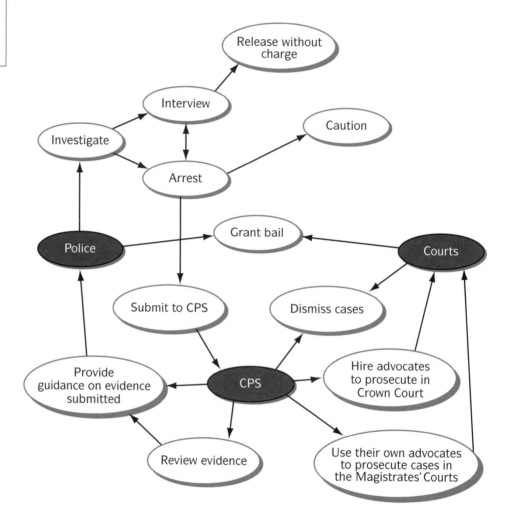

What happens pre-trial

The Courts' role pre-trial

The courts are clearly interested in reducing the number of cases they have to hear. There are a number of costs involved in every court case:

- financial costs of professional legal advice
- taxpayers' costs in running the Criminal Justice System
- the emotional cost to victims and defendants and their families
- costs of custodial sentences if the case goes to conviction and sentencing
- time wasted in calling witnesses and jurors.

There are a number of ways that the Criminal Justice System (CJS) filters cases out. We have already looked at two: the initial investigation by the police and the assessment of the CPS on whether to proceed. The courts also play their part.

Every criminal case starts at the Magistrates' Court and, depending on whether it is *summary*, triable *either way* or *indictable*, it remains at the first level or moves up to the Crown Court.

Summary offences are the most minor cases. They include drunk and disorderly conduct and minor public nuisance issues. Other summary offences include many driving offences such speeding, drink driving and driving without a licence or insurance. Minor assault charges and criminal damage that amount to less than £5000 are also summary offences. These cases are dealt with relatively quickly. A summons is sent to the accused, who is then asked to appear in front of the Magistrates' Court at a specified time. If a guilty plea is lodged, a summary of the facts is read to the court. The defence solicitor may make a statement explaining any background facts relevant to the defendant's actions. The statement by the defence solicitor is known as a **plea in mitigation**. This may shape the magistrates' sentencing of the defendant.

Offences either way are those which can be heard before a Magistrates' Court or a Crown Court. The defendant appears before the magistrates and then is asked how he or she pleads, guilty or not guilty. If there is sufficient evidence for a Crown Court trial, the case is committed to the Crown Court. These are known as *committal proceedings*. This is a way the magistrates can filter out cases which should not go further up the system to the Crown Court and direct those which should.

The defence will try to prove that no case exists if they want the case to be heard in the Magistrates' Court or be dismissed completely.

The magistrates will read the evidence that is produced against the accused and make a decision. If they feel that there is no case to answer, the accused will be free to go. If more evidence is gathered at a later stage, the process may start all over again and the accused may be sent to the Crown Court for trial by jury.

Indictable offences are the most serious of all criminal cases. They are now quickly transferred to the Crown Court by order of the **Crime and Disorder Act 1998**. The court will then hear evidence and the plea of the defendant and decide whether there is a case to answer. This process of identifying the key aspects of the case is known as a *plea and directions hearing*. If the defendant pleads guilty, a judge will hear the case and decide sentence. If the defendant pleads not guilty, the case will go before a jury who will listen to the facts and produce a verdict. If the jury decides on a guilty verdict, the judge sentences the defendant. If the jury has found the defendant not guilty, he or she is discharged.

The procedure is designed to protect suspects from unnecessary court proceedings and ensure that the most expensive court practice does not try irrelevant cases.

2 Bail

At any point after being arrested by the police, the accused can apply for bail. This means the accused person is free to go but promises to return at a later point to a police station or a court. The police or the court can offer bail. The **Bail Act 1976** indicates a 'presumption' that the person will receive the right to bail.

Reasons for bail

The criminal process can be long and bureaucratic. There are witness statements to be taken and court records to be completed; solicitors may have to talk to barristers or seek other advice, and the court itself may not have a convenient free date for many weeks, if not months. Even when a defendant has been found

Bail

guilty, there may be pre-sentence reports to be completed to give those sentencing a better picture of the defendant's background. What should be done with the accused? The presumption in English law is that the defendant is innocent before proved guilty. Even if guilty, the defendant may not receive a custodial sentence if there are extenuating circumstances. It would be very unfair if an innocent person were held in jail awaiting the chance for the prosecution to prove him guilty. The answer to this dilemma is bail.

Refusal of bail

Unless there are goods reasons for refusal, the **Bail Act 1976** presumes that bail will be granted. Reasons for denial include:

- suspicion that the accused would fail to return as promised
- suspicion that the accused would commit further offences whilst they were free on bail
- suspicion that the accused would interfere with the course of the criminal enquiry or intimidate potential court witnesses
- fear that the accused might be intimidated, injured or killed if released on bail
- no secure address for the accused (although **bail hostels** can be used in these cases).

Conditions associated with bail

Bail is often offered with conditions.

- The person may be ordered not to approach or communicate with the victim, or even go into the locality where the victim of the alleged crime lives.
- The accused person may have to report daily or weekly to a police station to prove they have not absconded, or their passport may be confiscated to prevent escape overseas.
- An electronic tag may have to be worn around the ankle to let the authorities know where the accused is.

Sureties

If it is feared that a person may not return after being bailed, the court may ask for some form of security. Someone who is prepared to pay the court a sum of money if the accused fails to return is known as a *surety*.

The amount of money required for this guarantee depends on:

- the crime itself
- the quality of evidence against the accused
- the character of the accused
- whether the accused ever abused the bail process before.

If an accused person does not turn up when asked to, the surety pays the money agreed. It is not paid in advance. This is different from many other countries, which demand money before the defendant is released. A recent case involving some British plane-spotters who were arrested in Greece on spying charges highlighted the differences. Each of the accused had to pay £9000 before they were released on bail.

The prosecution may use the **Bail (Amendment) Act 1993** to appeal against the award of bail if they consider there are reasons that the accused will prove unreliable and fail to appear later. This is normally on cases where the maximum penalty is five years or more. It is felt that the longer the possible imprisonment, the more chance there is of the accused not returning.

There is a problem here of balancing the needs of the two sides. The criminal court system wants to process offenders, and the general public want to be protected against potentially dangerous people. The offenders, however, want their right to freedom until a court of law proves them guilty. Many people **held on remand** are later found not guilty or have such short prison sentences that they are immediately released from custody. The courts therefore have to be careful in balancing up the rights of each party.

3 Mode of trial

The Magistrates' Court plays a vital part in deciding the mode of trial relevant for each offence. At the moment the defendant has a degree of choice in 'either way' offences, although proposals from the Auld Report may reduce this choice. For the convenience of the system, cases are classified into one of three categories: summary, either way or indictable. The first is heard in the Magistrates', the second either in the Magistrates' or the Crown Court, and the third only in the Crown Court.

Magistrates' trials

Trials in the Magistrates' Court are relatively quick. They involve:

● reading out a summary of the facts

● seeking a plea of guilty or not guilty from the accused

● hearing arguments put forward by prosecution and defence

● a verdict from the magistrates if there has been a plea of not guilty

● sentencing, or a request for further information to help with sentencing

● release if not guilty.

Crown Court trial

The Crown Court process is more complex. It consists of the following steps.

1 Prosecution lawyers outline their case against the defendant.

2 Prosecution witnesses are called to give evidence against the defendant.

3 Defence **cross-examines** the prosecution evidence.

4 Defence lawyers outline their case in support of the defendant.

5 Defence witnesses called to support the defendant.

6 Prosecution lawyers cross-examine the defence evidence.

7 The prosecution, defence and judge **sum up** the case.

8 The jury is brought to a private room where they can speak about the case. They have to reach a verdict based on the evidence. The verdict should be unanimous, but if they cannot do this within 2 hours and 10 minutes the judge can accept an 11–1 or a 10–2 majority. See Module 2 Unit 5 for more discussion of juries.

9 If the defendant is found guilty, the defence make a case for leniency before sentencing by the judge.

10 If the defendant is found not guilty, they are free to leave the court.

Cross-examination

Double jeopardy means that a defendant who is found not guilty cannot be tried for that same offence again, even if more evidence appears at a later stage possibly proving his or her guilt. The Government is thinking of taking this right away.

1 Do you think double jeopardy should be abandoned in the interests of justice?

2 Why do you think such a rule exists?

4 Committal proceedings

Committal proceedings move triable either way cases from the Magistrates' Court to the Crown Court after the magistrates have listened to the case against the defendant. The law covering committal proceedings is contained in the **Magistrates' Courts Act 1980**:

● Section 6 (1) of the **Magistrates' Courts Act 1980** requires all prosecution evidence to be read and considered by the magistrates before they consider whether there is a case to answer at the Crown Court.

● Under Section 6 (2) of the **Magistrates' Courts Act 1980** the defendant is automatically referred to the Crown Court with the permission of the defence lawyer. In this case the magistrates do not formally consider the evidence.

5 Jurisdictions of Magistrates', Youth and Crown Courts

Magistrates' Court jurisdiction

The word *jurisdiction* means the power the court has to deal with a particular legal matter. Some powers of jurisdiction overlap between courts. For example, either way offences can be heard in the Magistrates' Court or the Crown Court.

Magistrates have jurisdiction over all minor criminal cases (summary cases) and those either way offences where it is decided they should be heard in the Magistrates' Court. They also have jurisdiction over some civil matters.
See Module 1 Unit 1 for further information.

The Magistrates' Court is the first port of call for all criminal offences. It acts as a filter for the Crown Court, preventing unsuitable cases going forward, and tries 98 per cent of criminal cases. It deals with two types of cases:

● *Summary cases* involving custodial sentences of up to 6 months
(or 12 months if two offences are heard together) and a fine of £5000.

● *Triable either way* if it is decided that the case will be heard in the Magistrates' rather than the Crown Court.

Jurisdiction of Magistrates' Courts

The magistrates hear all cases and send serious *indictable offences* to the Crown Court. This is known as *mode of trial proceedings*. The details of this are about to change as a direct result of the Auld Report. Many more cases will be heard in the Magistrates' Courts, and 'middling offences' may now be heard in a new type of court with one district judge and two magistrates.

Other functions relating to the criminal element of their court work include:

● hearing bail applications

● issuing arrest warrants to the police

● issuing search warrants to the police.

Youth Court jurisdiction

The Youth Court has jurisdiction over most criminal cases involving young people aged between 10 and 17.

The Youth Court is part of the Magistrates' Court and is staffed by lay magistrates who have specialized training. This court hears most criminal cases involving offenders between the ages of 10 and 17. Very serious criminal charges such as murder and manslaughter are dealt with in the Crown Court. A young person may also appear in an adult court if they are charged as a co-defendant with an adult.

The proceedings in the youth court are less obviously formal than in other criminal courts. Parents or guardians of offenders younger than 16 must attend the hearings, unless there are very exceptional circumstances. The court has the power to order attendance by parents or guardians. Press reporting is restricted, and there is no public gallery. The bench must have at least one female and one male magistrate.

Crown Court jurisdiction

The Crown Court has jurisdiction over indictable criminal cases or either way offences referred up from the Magistrates' Court.

The Crown Court deals with the most serious criminal offences and also hears appeals from the Magistrates' Court. Circuit Judges or recorders staff the Court.

6 Appeals

An appeal is a challenge to a decision made by a court. The convicted defendant may be able to lodge an appeal against conviction or sentence. In some cases the prosecution may lodge an appeal if they believe the sentence handed down to the defendant is inadequate or that a point of law needs clarification. Once a person is acquitted there can be no appeal against this decision under double jeopardy rules.

There are three important concepts that are relevant when examining decisions made by courts and whether an appeal is relevant. Each is described by a Latin phrase:

- *Audi alterum partem:* both sides should be heard.
- *Nemo judex in causa sua:* no one should be allowed to judge their own case.
- *Ultra vires:* no organization should act beyond its powers.

Appeal from a trial of a summary offence

There are two main ways an appeal from a Magistrates' Court is dealt with.

- An appeal from a summary trial conducted in a Magistrates' Court is normally to the Crown Court. A judge will sit with two magistrates to hear the appeal. The Crown Court may vary the sentence or can pass the case back to the Magistrates' Court for further consideration. The Crown Court will normally give an opinion to guide the magistrates.
- An appeal can also be made to the Queen's Bench Divisional Court to get advice on a point of law or of legal procedure. The case can go to the House of Lords if there is no solution at this level. The prosecution or defence can use this route for appeal.

Appeal from a trial of an indictable offence

An appeal from the Crown Court has two main possibilities.

- An appeal can go to the Court of Appeal (Criminal Division). The appeal can consider whether the conviction is unsafe. The Court of Appeal can also consider the sentence and vary this if it thinks appropriate.
- An appeal can go to the House of Lords if, in the opinion of the Court of Appeal, a general point of law is raised through the case. The case can go to the House of Lords only if either the Court of Appeal or the House of Lords is of the opinion that this is the best place to find a solution.

7 The role of the Criminal Cases Review Commission

In response to pressure from a number of sources, the Government established an independent body, the Criminal Cases Review Commission (CCRC), to consider possible miscarriages of justice. The cases of the Birmingham Six and the Guildford Four had brought the system into disrepute in the eyes of some people. The **Home Secretary** had been responsible for reviews and referrals to the Court of Appeal. It was felt that holding a political post might affect the Home Secretary's views when high-profile cases were inspected. The CCRC is substantially free from Government pressure. The CCRC can query convictions and sentences and ask for the case to go back to court.

The main functions of the CCRC are:

- to consider suspected miscarriages of justice
- to arrange investigations of the case, if appropriate
- to refer cases to the Court of Appeal if there are grounds uncovered by the investigation of the case
- to settle outstanding issues on request from the Court of Appeal
- to give advice when the Home Secretary is considering a Royal Pardon
- to refer cases to the Home Secretary for consideration of a Royal Pardon.

Web activity

Look up www.ccrc.gov.uk and identify the key functions of the CCRC and reasons for its creation.

The CCRC has a huge workload and insufficient resources to deal with the task. Whether a case is taken up and processed is very much a matter of luck. Justice is served by having the CCRC, but at a very slow pace.

Criminal Cases Review Commission

Revision checklist

1 The police investigate the offence and pass papers to the Crown Prosecution Service, who decide whether to prosecute or not.

2 Cautions are used by the police to warn offenders of their behaviour.

3 All criminal cases start in the Magistrates' Court. All *summary* and some *either way* offences are heard there, too.

4 More serious offences are sent to Crown Court. They are known as *indictable offences*.

5 Bail is covered by the **Bail Act 1976** and allows people to go free if they agree to come back to court or to a police station in the future.

6 Jurisdiction means the cases courts hear and their power:

 ● The Magistrates' Court hears more minor offences, known as summary offences.

 ● The Youth Courts deal with 10–17 year-olds.

 ● Crown Courts deal with the most serious criminal cases, called indictable offences.

7 Appeals involve challenging the decision of a court. Appeals can be made against sentence, conviction or point of law.

8 Appeal from a summary offence in the Magistrates' Court goes to the Crown Court or the Queen's Bench Division of the High Court.

9 Appeal from an indictable offence in the Crown Court goes to the Court of Appeal (Criminal Division), or to the House of Lords on a point of law.

10 The Criminal Cases Review Commission (CCRC) looks into possible miscarriages of justice.

Quick revision questions

1 What is the role of the police in a criminal case?

2 What is a caution?

3 What is the main function of the Crown Prosecution Service?

4 What are grounds for refusing bail?

5 How is a case tried in a Magistrates' Court?

6 How is a case tried in the Crown Court?

7 What are committal proceedings?

8 What does the word *jurisdiction* mean?

9 How does the appeal system work?

10 What specific cases led to the creation of the Criminal Cases Review Commission?

Exam questions

1 **a** Outline the main steps in a criminal trial. [20 marks]

  b Evaluate the need for an effective appeals procedure in the criminal courts system. [25 marks]

Exam answer guide

1 **a** Outline means 'give a brief description of'. Points to include:

✓ Committal proceedings

✓ Plea and directions hearing

✓ Prosecution outlines case

✓ Witnesses called for prosecution

✓ Cross-examination

✓ Defence does the same as above

✓ Everyone sums up

✓ Jury returns verdict.

b Why do you need an appeals procedure?:

✓ Miscarriages take place

✓ Witnesses can be unreliable

✓ Sentences are custodial

✓ Jury or judge may make mistakes

✓ Prosecution or defence may not do their job properly

✓ To give public faith in the system

✓ Fair deal for defendants.

The system of law and order is very important to ordinary citizens and society. It must be fair and seen to be fair. Mistakes can be made so an appeals procedure shows that the system is big enough to admit error quickly and effectively. The key word to look out for here is *evaluate*. This means giving your opinion based on your analysis of the issues. This is where you can gain high marks.

Principles of sentencing

Key points

1 The aims of sentencing
2 The purpose and effects of sentencing
3 Reoffending rates

Why do I need to know about the principles of sentencing?

Principles of sentencing go the heart of the Criminal Justice System. Knowledge gained in this unit can be used across the syllabus to give depth to questions asked about the Criminal Justice System, Government funding of legal services, judges and the power of the appeals system. You need to know about present structures and policies, but also about the possible impact of the Government-initiated Halliday Report, which has examined the area of sentencing policy.

The deterrent

1 The aims of sentencing

A criminal offence is one where the state, on behalf of the community, hopes to send a clear signal that a type of behaviour is unacceptable. Criminal offences are viewed as serious violations of what is commonly agreed to be normal or acceptable behaviour.

There are two principal schools of thought on punishment – the retributive view and the rehabilitative view.

The retributive view

Retributive punishment is about punishment for wrongdoing; it is about revenge on behalf of the victim and society. The saying 'An eye for an eye' sums up this approach.

Someone who supports retribution does not look at the circumstances of the defendant. Only what the defendant has done is considered. The more serious the crime, the more serious the punishment must be.

The retributive idea appeals because of its simplicity. The world of retribution is straightforward. The offender is punished severely and as a result does not reoffend because he or she wants to avoid future punishment.

The rehabilitative view

The rehabilitative view sees punishment as fulfilling a useful purpose for the individual, and hopefully for the community. If an individual can become a more useful member of society and has something to give, he or she will be less likely to reoffend and create further victims.

Aims of sentencing – punishment

In 1990 the Conservative Government produced a White Paper called *Crime, Justice and Protecting the Public*. This paper called for 'just deserts', which meant that the punishment should fit the crime.

Some people have argued that the economic and social standing of the defendant must have a part to play here, and therefore their circumstances must be taken into consideration. It might be argued that an affluent defendant commits different types of crime and has the ability to pay fines. The poorer defendant is more likely to commit crimes that attract harsher custodial punishments.

Does punishment work in the long run? The Conservative Party and the Labour Party are now both happy to be seen as 'tough on crime', which presumably means more frequent and longer prison sentences.

Group activity

'Tough on crime and tough on the causes of crime' (Tony Blair, Labour Prime Minister)

'Prison works' (Michael Howard, former Conservative Home Secretary)

1 What are the key differences between these two views?

2 How would law and order policies operate under each perspective?

Aims of sentencing – deterrence

The view of the retributionist school of thought is that a harsh and uncompromising sentence will send a signal to other potential offenders and deter those who have had to suffer such a punishment from offending again. There are some questions that arise with this system:

- Is it punishment that is the deterrent, or the fear of being caught? If an offender believed there was a 98 per cent chance of being caught, but there was a relatively light sentence, would they commit the crime?

- Some crimes are really 'one-offs' which the defendant would never commit again. Is it fair in such circumstances to punish harshly? Does it send a signal to others? Is it relevant to others?

- Many serious crimes are ones where the offender is under a great deal of pressure. Can a person think rationally about deterrent punishments in a very tense and emotionally upsetting situation?

- Does the potential offender know what the sentence is? The offender cannot be deterred by something they know nothing about!

There is some evidence that the deterrent effect becomes less powerful for habitual criminals. If an offender has been imprisoned a number of times, the punishment seems to lack its sting. The habitual criminal may become accustomed to a 'criminal way of life'. For such a person the fear of a custodial sentence is reduced and the offender sees prison as 'an occupational hazard'.

Younger offenders cause particular concern. If the cycle of crime can be broken early in a person's life there may be more hope for them and society. The present system has a series of steps that start with a caution or reprimand and rise through fines, probation, and eventually to custodial sentences.

Some people argue that a 'short, sharp shock' at the outset of criminal behaviour would work as a profound deterrent. This line has been tried in both the United States and the United Kingdom, with poor results. The **Criminal Justice Act 1982** brought these measures in with so-called 'boot camps'. These 'camps' were military-style detention centres with lots of drilling and hard exercise. The 'boot camps' were abandoned with the **Criminal Justice Act 1988**.

Deterrent?

The aims of sentencing – rehabilitation

The aim of rehabilitation is to change the behaviour of offenders. This may happen if:

● offenders see the pain and damage they have caused through their anti-social behaviour

● educational and training facilities have provided an alternative career path for offenders.

This approach is seen as particularly important for young offenders, who may be able to use skills learned in prison for useful employment on release.

This approach requires additional resources. Unfortunately prison budgets are not seen as a priority when Governments have to make choices about spending.

Although is may seem as if the rehabilitative approach is an effective philosophy, there are some criticisms:

- It assumes that the problem is with the individual rather than the society.

- Poorer individuals may be treated more intensively than comfortable middle-class offenders who have 'just made a terrible mistake'.

- The process of rehabilitation involves stripping away the privacy of the offender in group therapy sessions and asking prying questioning about background and family life.

Aims of sentencing – protection of society

The usual method of protecting citizens from violent or dangerous individuals is by administering long prison sentences. Murder automatically triggers a life sentence. Rape and other crimes of violence also carry long prison sentences on conviction. If an offender commits a second violent or sexual offence, a life sentence is automatically given. This has been the result of recent legislation, the **Crime (Sentences) Act 1997**. Given that the cost of a prisoner 'kept inside' for a year amounts to over £25 000, prison is a very expensive way of protecting the public.

Group activity

Many victims and their families applaud the retributive aim. It meets their need for revenge through punishment of the defendant.

1 Do you think retribution is a civilized way to sentence criminals?

2 What factors might a court take into account to give a fairer 'punishment'?

2 Aims and effects of sentencing

Sentencing has many aims, including retribution, deterrence, rehabilitation, and protection of society. Everybody wants freedom from being victims of crime and also freedom from fear of crime. Does sentencing meet its aims? What effects come from imposing sentences on offenders?

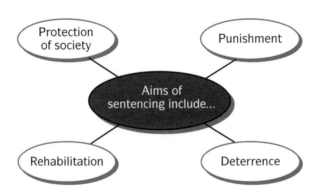

Aims of sentencing

Effects on prisoners

Custodial sentences may introduce the less serious offender to life-long criminals. The 'university of crime' may give some inmates ideas for new and creative offences and remove the taboo of offending.

On the other hand, prison may traumatize. The conditions inside many of Her Majesty's Prisons are extremely basic. The Chief Inspector of Prisons has levelled damning criticism on particular jails around the country for lack of sanitation, exercise facilities and activities. The easy, comfortable prison life depicted by some tabloid newspapers is far from the brutal reality in a number of prisons.

Effects on young offenders

One of the most tragic effects of custodial sentences is the increased risk of suicide amongst young offenders. It may be the first time they have been separated from families, friends and community. They are placed into severe conditions where bullying and intimidation often take place. For some the pressure becomes too great, and suicide or attempted suicide occurs. Some institutions for young offenders have come under intense scrutiny for the unsupportive regimes they foster.

Effects on employment prospects

After prison, employment may prove more difficult to secure. Many employers view with suspicion people who have been in prison. The effects of the sentence do not end when the prisoner leaves the cell. This, of course, increases the

Young offender

likelihood of more offending. With no stable income and no prospects, some ex-prisoners have nothing left to lose.

Effect on prisoners' families

Custodial sentences put great pressure on partners and children of prisoners. There are support groups to provide help, but the imprisonment of a husband or mother puts many families under enormous financial and emotional strain.

One worrying statistic is the alarming rise in the number of women being put into prison. There was a 28 per cent rise between 2000 and 2001. Some prisons are flexible when dealing with mothers with very young children, but older children often lose out.

Web activity

One of the biggest women's prisons, at Holloway in London, has a special unit for mothers with babies. Find the website for HM Prisons and explore the Prison Service's philosophy on its care for female inmates: www.hmprisonservice.gov.uk.

The National Association for Care and Rehabilitation of Offenders (NACRO)

The National Association for the Care and Rehabilitation of Offenders (NACRO) is a national organization which supports prisoners and their families. A key way to reduce crime is to support offenders when they come out of prison. If they are helped with housing and employment, ex-offenders may feel they have a stake in the community and it is hoped they have less incentive to reoffend. NACRO works with prisoners both before and after release.

Web activity

See www.nacro.org.uk for further information on NACRO's aims and services.

3 Reoffending rates

Sentencing should impact on crime in several different ways.

- Imprisonment should reduce more serious crime, because criminals are in jail and not on the street.
- Reform and rehabilitation should be producing potential offenders who consider their victims and resist offending.
- Reparation, where victims get compensation from the offender, should discourage some potential criminals.

It might be more accurate, however, to talk about *reconviction* rather than reoffending rates, since we have no evidence if reoffenders are not caught. There is some alarming statistical evidence about reconviction rates. The figures on page 59 were taken from *Prison Statistics, England and Wales 1999*.

Length of sentence and reconviction rates

Seventy per cent of all offenders released in 1996 offended again within five years. However, the following differences were shown in the statistics.

Reconviction rates were higher for those serving shorter sentences than for those serving longer sentences. Those reconvicted within two years of discharge in 1996 were:

● sentence up to 12 months: 60 per cent

● sentence over 12 months but less than four years: 53 per cent

● sentence over four years but less than ten years: 31 per cent

● sentence over ten years but less than life imprisonment: 29 per cent

● life sentence: 5 per cent.

Age and reconviction rates

Age is another factor which determines the level of reconviction rates. The following evidence suggests a strong relationship. Reconviction rates within two years for males released in 1996 were:

● 14–16 year-olds: 85 per cent

● 17–20 year-olds: 74 per cent

● above 20 years old: 76 per cent.

These figures are particularly worrying. If younger offenders are returning to young offender institutions or prisons, a pattern is being set which may be difficult to break out of.

The costs of long-term custodial sentences are astronomic. A prisoner who spends 15 years in prison will cost the taxpayer approximately £375 000. There are clearly better ways to spend the money.

Index card revision
Make notes of the key figures in the reconviction statistics supplied by *Prison Statistics*.

Nature of crime and reconviction rates

The statistics indicate that offenders imprisoned for certain types of offences have a much higher reconviction rate than others. In 1996 the following rates for reconviction within two years were:

● burglary: 76 per cent

● theft and handling: 71 per cent

● robbery: 55 per cent

● fraud and forgery: 24 per cent

● sexual offences: 19 per cent.

These figures, of course, cross-reference with age of offender and length of sentence, so the picture can be difficult to put together.

Breaking old habits can be hard

Group activity

Using the statistics on length of sentence, age of offender and nature of offence, give reasons for the variations in reconviction rates.

Exam tip

Quote reports such as the Halliday Report in your work.

Halliday Report on sentencing

A major review into the effects of punishments was published in July 2001. The Halliday Report investigated the effectiveness of the sentencing framework for England and Wales. It attempted to suggest improvements in the current arrangements, which were seen as unsatisfactory by many people.

In all, there were 55 major recommendations, including:

- the targeting of persistent offenders
- research into the contribution of sentencing to crime reduction
- increasing the severity of the sentence when the offender has recent convictions
- using imprisonment only as a last resort
- a review of mandatory minimum sentences so that judges could have more flexibility.

The Report's author, John Halliday, concluded that the present use of short prison sentences is not working, and that the problem of persistent offenders is not being tackled.

The Halliday Report

Group activity

The prison population of England and Wales on 23 November 2001 totalled
68 357. That figure includes:

- 53 779 adult male prisoners
- 3469 adult female prisoners
- 10 539 young male offenders
- 570 young female offenders.

A young offender is someone between the ages of 15 and 21.

1 How do you account for the numbers and the differences between the groups?

2 Do you think the trends will change over the next 20 years?

Web activity

The Halliday Report contains a vast array of data and charts on the effects of
sentencing policy. See the full document on the Home Office website:
www.homeoffice.gov.uk/cpd/sou/sfrleaft.

Revision checklist

1 Two main schools of thought on sentencing:

- retributive – look at the crime and punish accordingly; just deserts: an eye for an eye

- rehabilitative – look at all the circumstances and possibly reform offender. Try to make punishment achieve something.

2 Aims of sentencing include: punishment, deterrence, rehabilitation, protection of society and reparation.

3 Sentencing will affect: prisoners and their futures, young offenders in particular, and families of prisoners.

4 NACRO is the key organization supporting prisoners.

5 Seventy per cent of offenders are reconvicted within five years.

6 Those serving shorter sentences are more likely to be reconvicted.

7 Younger offenders are more likely to reoffend.

8 Burglars are over three times more likely to reoffend than sex offenders.

9 The Halliday Report investigated views on sentencing framework.

10 The Halliday Report suggests that the problem of persistent offenders needs to be tackled and mentions doubts over effectiveness of short prison sentences.

Quick revision questions

1 What is a criminal offence?

2 What are the two views on sentencing?

3 What are the main aims of sentencing?

4 What was the 'short, sharp shock'?

5 What are the key effects on prisoners of a custodial sentence?

6 What is NACRO?

7 How does length of sentence affect reconviction rates?

8 How does age affect reconviction rates?

9 How does type of crime affect reconviction rates?

10 What is the Halliday Report?

Exam question

1 a What are the main aims of sentencing policy? [25 marks]

b Do prison sentences work? [20 marks]

Exam answer guide

1 a Main aims of sentencing policy include:

✓ Punishment

✓ Deterrence

✓ Rehabilitation

✓ Protection of society

✓ Reparation.

You will have very little time to explore all of these, so choose two and develop some points in depth. Mention the others in your concluding paragraph.

b Quote Michael Howard, the former Conservative Home Secretary, when he said, 'Prison works', but then look at the evidence that reconviction rates range from 85 per cent reconviction rate for 14–16 year-olds to five per cent for life-sentence servers. It is a very mixed picture and seems to depend more on your political outlook than on any firm, indisputable facts.

Powers of the courts

Key points

1 Custodial sentences
2 Community sentences
3 Fines
4 Discharges
5 Compensation
6 Other powers

Why do I need to know about the powers of the courts?

Questions on the powers of courts will expect you to be aware of the range of options the courts have to punish offenders. Sentencing is an important part of the criminal justice system and has effects on the prison system, the probation service and hopefully on crime levels. It is therefore important that you know the key legislative developments of recent years and whether they have made any difference to reconviction rates. The Auld Report promises to redistribute powers amongst the two criminal courts and the Halliday Report has explored

The judge

sentencing. This unit therefore ties in closely with the units on magistrates and on barristers, solicitors and judges.

1 Custodial sentences

Custodial sentences involve depriving the convicted person of their liberty and freedom. This is the most severe punishment the criminal justice system uses and has a major impact on the defendant and their family. It is therefore used with care, and all other possibilities are considered first. A court can only pass a custodial sentence when:

- the offence was so serious that the only response could be a custodial sentence
- the case involved violence or a sexual element and it is thought the public needs protection.

Details of sentencing are outlined in the **Powers of Criminal Courts (Sentencing) Act 2000** (PCC). This piece of legislation is now the focus for virtually all sentencing by the courts.

The judge decides the length of sentence, although there is guidance available. The sentence depends on:

- the seriousness of the offence
- whether the public needs protection from the actions of a violent or sexual offender.

The way that an offender is punished is partly dependent on the political complexion of the Government. The last Conservative Government believed that prison was a very effective option. The present Labour Government has gone along the same path to a certain extent, although it has toughened up non-custodial options to allow more use. The current view is that punishment should carry messages of:

- Deterrence: the actual offender and the potential offender should both be aware of the stiff penalties for breaking the law.
- The punishment should reflect the seriousness of the crime. A more serious crime gets a more severe punishment.

Some offences, such as murder, carry **mandatory sentences**. This means that, no matter what the circumstances surrounding the case, each murder conviction carries a compulsory life sentence.

Group activity

Murder carries a life sentence *no matter what the circumstances* of the case and regardless of the personal circumstances of the defendant.

1 Can you think of some examples where the judge should be given some flexibility over the sentence he or she passes?

2 What benefits come from having one sentence for all?

Link

A number of other orders applicable to young offenders are community-based. We will look at these in more detail in Section 2, on community sentences.

Young offenders

Special consideration is always given to young offenders (aged between 10 and 17) when they appear in front of a court and when sentence is passed. Their cases are dealt with thoroughly since it is important that they are kept out of the criminal justice system if at all possible.

Powers the courts have include *supervision orders*. The young offender can be put into a secure local authority unit (Section 63, PCC). They are held in custody but are given educational support and training. They normally have their own room, which is more comfortable and homely than the typical prison cell. The numbers in each unit are small, but the problem still exists of relatively inexperienced offenders sometimes mixing with more experienced offenders and learning bad habits from them.

Concurrent and consecutive

Custodial sentences may be served concurrently or consecutively. *Concurrent sentences* are all served at the same time. Therefore if a series of five offences is carried out which each has a ten-year term, only ten years will be served by the prisoner.

$$10 + 10 + 10 + 10 + 10 = 10$$

Concurrent sentences

If the same five sentences were consecutive, then a total of 50 years would be served.

$$10 + 10 + 10 + 10 + 10 = 50$$

Consecutive sentences

Web activity

Explore the latest statistics for the prison population on the Home Office site and the HM Prisons site. See if you can identify any recent trends in totals and within the different groups. You can find the sites at www.homeoffice.gov.uk and www.hmprisonservice.gov.uk.

2 Community sentences

A custodial sentence is seen as the most severe punishment to be handed down to the offender. Some offences do not require such a harsh penalty. One option available to the courts is a *community sentence*. Such sentences are served in the community and not in prison. They do, however, interfere with the offender's day-to-day life. He or she is required to carry out tasks and fulfil certain duties. If not, the offender can be brought back to court. Community sentences are only possible if the offence may have warranted a prison sentence. There are many types of community sentences, including the following.

Community Rehabilitation Order (probation order)

The offender is required to see a probation officer regularly for between six months and three years. The probation officer gives guidance to the offender and monitors their progress. There may be conditions attached to the probation order, which might include:

- the offender living at a particular address
- the offender going for counselling or other medical treatment to support their rehabilitation
- the offender not seeing certain people or types of people; these could include known criminals.

The Government has recently changed the name of a probation order to a Community Rehabilitation Order (Section 41, PCC). This clearly signals the hope that the process will reform the offender and change their behaviour.

Unfortunately some see the issue of a Community Rehabilitation Order as a soft option. It is offered instead of prison, so in one sense it is a lot less drastic. The aim, however, is a mix of punishment and rehabilitation. Prison provides a far less effective environment for rehabilitation of the offender.

Community Punishment Order (Community Service Order)

Community punishment orders (Section 46, PCC) are meant to carry an element of punishment but also involve a degree of rehabilitation and of compensation to the community. The offender is required to carry out tasks such as decorating the homes of the elderly, helping with local environmental projects and supporting charities and churches with their good works. The name of these orders has changed to underline the punishment element. The total time involved is between 40 and 240 hours.

Community Punishment and Rehabilitation Order (Combination Order)

Community Punishment and Rehabilitation Orders (Section 51, PCC) are a combination of a punishment order and a rehabilitation order – a stick and a carrot. The offender would have to attend probation interviews to monitor progress and also fulfil some community work.

Curfew Order

The offender agrees to be at a particular place for an agreed number of hours. Often the offender must be at home between 7pm and 7am. Electronic tagging enforces the order. A tag is attached to the offender's ankle, and if they move from the agreed location the police are notified. This is an infringement of liberties, but the alternative is to be held in custody. Most offenders, given the choice, go for tagging (Section 37, PCC).

Exclusion Order

Offenders may be banned from certain areas where they have offended or may come in contact with those who may encourage them to offend. Exclusion orders (Section 40, PCC) can last for two years if the offender is over 16 and up to three months if under 16.

Anti-social Behaviour Order

The **Crime and Disorder Act 1998** made possible anti-social behaviour orders. These orders are intended for younger offenders aged over 10 who indulge in behaviour which causes concern to the local community. Yobbish behaviour and petty vandalism are the normal offences. Local authorities or the police seldom use these orders. There seem to be major problems about their enforcement and their effectiveness.

Drug Abstinence Order

Drug abstinence orders (Section 56, PCC) apply to class A drugs such as heroin. The offender is formally banned from taking these drugs for between six months and three years. The order is there to emphasize to the offender the will of the court in a more obvious way. Taking class A drugs is, of course, illegal at any time other than for authorized medical purposes.

Community sentences

Young offenders

Clearly courts are keen to impose community sentences rather than custodial sentences for young people. Community orders available for young offenders include the following types.

Action plan

The young offender has to become involved in set activities or avoid certain locations (Section 69, PCC).

Referral

The young offender may have to meet with a youth offender team to get advice and guidance.

Parental order

Parents/guardians can be ordered to take full responsibility for the offender for up to three years (Section 150, PCC) and be forced to attend counselling sessions to support them.

Parental orders

Index card revision

Make a set of revision cards showing the key elements of community-based sentencing.

Children under 10

Children under 10 are not criminally responsible, but there are powers to deal with them if they commit criminal offences. They can be put under the supervision of a social worker or be forced to see a member of the youth offending team. They can also be ordered to stay away from certain locations and to be kept indoors for certain times of the day or night (curfew).

3 Fines

Money that courts order offenders to pay as punishment for their crimes is paid to the state. The victim of the crime does not receive the money. If money is paid to the victim it is known as a *compensation order*.

A problem arises when deciding what level of fine to impose. The personal financial circumstances of the offender will make a difference. A custodial sentence would affect both in roughly the same way, but a fine might be of much less importance to a very rich person than to a poor person. If a fine is going to work as a punishment then the richer person should pay a much higher penalty. On the other hand, a person on Income Support who only has £40 per week to live on should expect a much smaller fine. The **Criminal Justice Act 1993** abolished the system that hoped to deal with this situation because of the many problems that arose.

The level of fines appropriate for each offence is listed in the legislation. It is up to magistrates and judges to use their common-sense when applying the punishment to offenders.

4 Discharges

Glossary

Crimes caused by some unusual situation may have this taken into account. The situation is also known as **extenuating circumstance** or **mitigating circumstance**.

Absolute discharge

If the court is satisfied that *no* punishment is appropriate, it may give an absolute discharge. This means that the offender is free to go and is not subject to any conditions.

An absolute discharge is given in circumstances when the offender has pleaded guilty or is found guilty. The court records the offence but nothing else happens to the offender. Absolute discharges are rare. They often involve cases where people have committed a criminal offence but have had strong justifying reasons to do so.

Conditional discharge

It is much more likely that the court will apply some conditions to the offender if they are released without formal punishment. The most common is that they are *bound over*. This means that if they commit another offence within a set time period (normally up to three years) they will be brought to court to face the new charges and the old ones again.

Fines have varied effects

5 Compensation

As mentioned earlier, fines go to the state rather than to the victim. There is, however, a method of forcing the offender to compensate the victim. These are known as *compensation orders* (Section 130, PCC). These can be imposed in addition to, or instead of, a custodial or community sentence. Compensation orders are an attempt at reparation for the victim – repair for the damage done.

Group activity

Recent guidelines given to magistrates give the following advice on compensation to be paid to the victim of a violent attack.

Graze: up to £50

Bruise: up to £75

Black eye: £100

Cut without scarring: £75–500

Loss of a tooth: £250–500 (£1000 for front tooth)

Broken nose: £750–1750

Fractured jaw: £2750

These relate to victims 20–35 years-old. More can be paid if the victim is older.

Comment on the amounts awarded.

6 Other powers

The mentally ill

The courts have also been given the power to deal with offenders who are mentally ill. The main philosophy is that offenders in this category will receive treatment rather than punishment.

Treatment orders

The offender may be required to receive treatment from his or her doctor or from the out-patient department of a hospital as part of his or her release from the court. This will be possible only if the court believes that this method of treatment is going to be effective.

Hospital orders

Hospital orders is when the offender is ordered to attend a hospital as an in-patient to receive appropriate treatment. Again, the courts must be satisfied that this is the most effective course of action for the offender. This may have to be considered if the offender has inadequate support in the community from family or friends.

Secure hospitals

If the patient is believed to be dangerous to himself or to others, he may be detained under section 41 of the **Mental Health Act 1983** and held in a secure hospital. This action is taken if the courts believe that the offender is a danger to the public. This order can be made only by the Crown Court. The offender may be detained in a secure hospital for a set period or for an indefinite period, depending on the severity of his or her mental condition.

Awards from public funds

One last power the courts have is to award small money gifts to members of the public if they have acted in a particularly heroic or community-spirited manner. The usual payment is £50 or £100. Local newspapers often tell the tale.

Revision checklist

1 Custodial sentences involve loss of liberty and freedom and are used as a last resort.

2 Custody is used when the offence was so serious that custody was the only option or the offence involved violence or a sexual element.

3 **Powers of Criminal Courts (Sentencing) Act 2000** (PCC) is the key piece of legislation concerning sentencing.

4 Young offenders are treated differently, although they can receive a range of punishments similar to those used for the adult offender.

5 The main community sentences are community rehabilitation orders, community punishment orders and community punishment and rehabilitation orders.

6 Other powers of the court include curfew orders, exclusion orders, anti-social behaviour orders and drug abstinence orders.

7 There are powers to compel parents/guardians to take responsibility for their children or face court action.

8 Fines are paid to the state and not to the victim of the offence. They may penalize the poor more than the rich.

9 Victims of crime can receive compensation via compensation orders.

10 The court has powers to order the treatment of mentally ill offenders, or even to put them into secure hospitals.

Quick revision questions

1 What key piece of legislation gives the court its sentencing powers?

2 What does the length of a sentence depend on?

3 How old are young offenders?

4 What is a supervision order?

5 What is the difference between a consecutive and a concurrent sentence?

6 What are the main types of community sentences?

7 Why do fines penalize the poor unfairly?

8 What is a conditional discharge?

9 What is a compensation order?

10 Which Act of Parliament allows the secure detention of a mentally ill person?

Exam questions

1 a What sentences do courts have at their disposal? [15 marks]

 b What sentences are most effective in preventing reconviction of
 offenders? [30 marks]

Exam answer guide

1 a The key sentences courts have include:
- ✓ Custodial sentences
- ✓ Community sentences
- ✓ Fines
- ✓ Curfews, exclusion orders and drug abstinence orders
- ✓ Absolute and conditional discharges.

Give a brief description of each. You do not have time to evaluate each so
move quickly onto part **b**, which requires more time and asks for higher-level
skills to be demonstrated.

 b This part of the question is asking you for an opinion. Choose two or
 three of your answers to **a** and develop points around the effectiveness
 of each. Support your points with arguments and any statistics you are
 able to give. The examiner is looking for thoughtful and analytical
 arguments followed by a reasoned conclusion.

Legal Personnel

Legal personnel

1 Judiciary

2 Barristers and solicitors

3 Crown Prosecution Service

Lay people in the legal system

4 Lay magistrates

5 Juries

Provision of legal services

6 Government funding

7 Advice agencies

8 Role of the legal profession

Legal personnel

Judiciary

Key points

1 Appointment
2 Tenure
3 Independence
4 Role, including judicial review and enforcement of human rights
5 Role of the Lord Chancellor
6 The Theory of Separation of Powers

Why do I need to know about the judiciary?

Examination questions on judges will require you to know the part played by
them in the legal system and how independent they are from the various
pressures placed upon them. Independence of the judiciary is a complex legal
and political situation. For insight into the thinking of the Government, get a
clear understanding of the **Human Rights Act 1998**. In theory this gives judges

The judges

enormous independence. This is one of the most important changes to hit the English legal system for many centuries. Be prepared to quote any relevant articles and assess the Act's impact when tackling essays on this subject.

1 Appointment

Selection and appointment

The Lord Chancellor plays a crucial role in the appointment of all judges.

Superior judges

Superior judges are those of High Court level and above. The Lord Chancellor's Department carries out most of the work of appointment. It collects information on suitable people and then approaches them to see if they want the job. This may involve the 'old boys' network' and possibly corrupts the process of selection.

The superior judges are:

- the Law Lords (Lords of Appeal Ordinary)
- the Lord Justices of Appeal
- High Court Judges

Inferior judges

Inferior judges are those below High Court level. The **Court and Legal Services Act 1990** has brought some important changes for the appointment of these judges. Posts are now advertised, and potential candidates apply for interview. The Lord Chancellor still has the final say.

The inferior judges are:

- Circuit Judges
- Recorders and Assistant Recorders
- District Judges
- Stipendiary magistrates/District Judges (Magistrates' Courts).

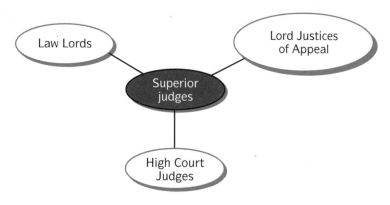

Superior judges

Senior judiciary

Senior **judiciary** are the most powerful posts in the legal system. The Lord Chancellor puts names forward, in order of preference, to the Prime Minister. The Prime Minister normally accepts the guidance of the Lord Chancellor on these matters.

The senior judiciary are:

- the Lord Chief Justice
- the Master of the Rolls
- the President of the Family Division
- the Vice-Chancellor of the Chancery Division.

Training of judges

The Judicial Studies Board is the formal organization that provides judges with their initial training and keeps them up to date with legal developments affecting their work. The judges are, of course, qualified barristers or solicitors, but the duties of a judge are very different from the experience gained as an advocate. The key training consists of a one-week residential course for newly appointed judges, followed up by refresher courses.

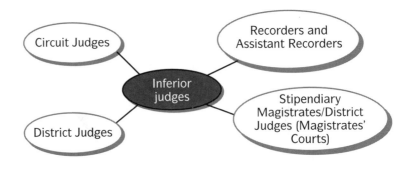

Inferior judges

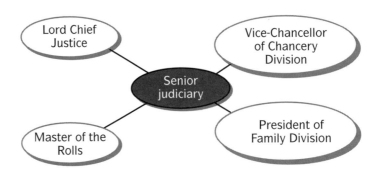

Senior judiciary

Type of judge	Superior or inferior	Type of cases	Type of court	Experience	Previous role
District Judge	Inferior	Minor criminal & civil	Magistrates' Court & County Court	Seven years	Barrister or Solicitor
Assistant Recorders & Recorders	Inferior	Criminal	Crown Court	Seven years	Barrister or Solicitor
Circuit Judge	Inferior	Difficult or valuable	County Court & Crown Court	Ten years	Barrister, Solicitor or District Judge
High Court Judge	Superior	Serious cases and appeals	High Court, Crown Court & Divisional Court	Ten years	Barrister or Solicitor
Lord Justices of Appeal	Superior	Appeal cases	Appeal Court & Divisional Court	At least Ten years	High Court Judge
Lords of Appeal Ordinary	Superior	Point of law	House of Lords	Ten years	Lord Justices of Appeal

Types of judges – who sits where

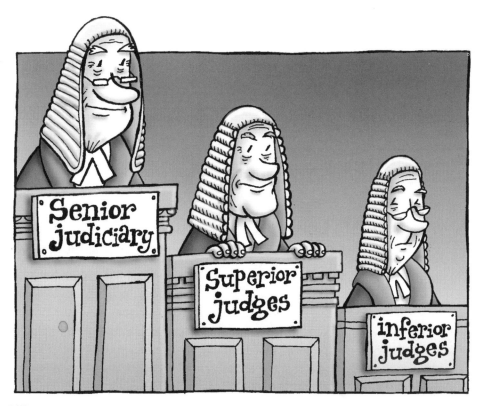

Different types of judges

2 Tenure

The word *tenure* refers to how secure a person's job is and how long it will last. Judges have very secure tenure because of the nature of their job. They need to know that decisions they make will not result in them being dismissed.

Dismissal

The dismissal of judges is very difficult. The system prides itself on having independence from pressures that might be put upon it by Government, the general public or other sources, and therefore judges need to feel secure in their posts.

Judges of the High Court and above (superior judges) are covered by the **Act of Settlement 1700**, which means that a judge can only be dismissed if both Houses of Parliament petition the monarch to do so. The last time this happened was in 1830.

Judges below High Court status (inferior judges) can be dismissed by the Lord Chancellor using the **Courts Act 1971**. Again, this power is rarely used. For those judges on fixed-term appointments, the Lord Chancellor may choose not to extend their contract.

In reality, the Lord Chancellor 'persuades' judges to retire or resign rather than push them out using formal procedures if he thinks they should not continue in their posts.

In addition to dismissal, the Lord Chancellor may remove a judge who has a permanent disability that means they cannot perform their duties.

3 Independence

Judges are clearly open to pressure from a variety of sources.

- First, the Government may wish to hear one verdict rather than another on important cases that affect its own policies and budgets. A recent ruling on the status of refugees into the UK may leave the Government open to huge compensation payments for illegal imprisonment. One must bear in mind, however, that the Lord Chancellor appoints senior judges in the first place, and that the Lord Chancellor is appointed by the Prime Minister.

- Multi-national companies and other lobbying groups can exert huge financial and political pressure. Judges must be free to make decisions on their

Dismissal of judges

interpretation of the facts and legal position. As part of this, however, they must be independent from any self-interest.

Legal case: *R v Pinochet (1998)*

General Pinochet, the former Chilean dictator, was held for extradition by the UK Government. One of the judges, Lord Hoffman, was seen as having an outside interest in the case through his association with human rights group Amnesty International.

The general public, supported by tabloid newspapers, can sometimes attempt to persuade judges to change their rulings on controversial and sensitive cases. The judges' independence gives them a firm foundation to resist such attention. Judges have immunity from being sued on judicial decisions.

Finally, the media, in all shapes and forms, can exert pressure on judges.

Group activity

The vast majority of judges have come from public schools and from wealthy backgrounds. They are usually white, middle-aged or older, and male.

Given the background of judges, can they really be independent and fair in their decision-making?

4 Role, including judicial review and enforcement of human rights

The role of judges

Judges are found in a variety of settings in the English legal system in both civil and criminal courts. Their key functions are:

- overseeing the conduct and procedures of the trial

- acting as legal experts when it comes to points of law

- in criminal cases, summing up the case, informing the jury of the relevant law and delivering a sentence if the jury finds the defendant guilty

- in civil cases, deciding the facts of the case and the verdict when no jury is sitting, and then deciding the remedy for the injured party.

Judicial Review

One of the most important functions of the judge is that of Judicial Review. This is carried out in the Queens's Bench Division of the High Court. The process involves examining the legality of a decision made by the Government, a court, by a public organization such as a local authority, or by any other large organization such as the Football Association. The Judicial Review can overturn the decision if it finds that the decision:

- involved an error of law

- was so unreasonable that no reasonable authority would have taken it

- goes against natural justice.

It will only act when there is no other option for appeal available.

The Human Rights Act

The Human Rights Act 1998 came into force in the English legal system in October 2000. From that date the provisions of the act were part of English Law and had to be interpreted and applied by English judges.

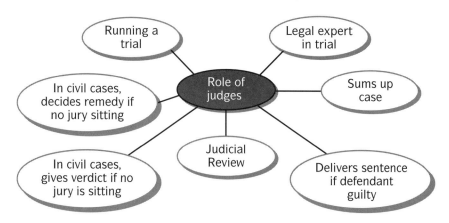

The role of judges

There are fourteen main articles to the act, of which the following may be of particular significance to the judiciary. People have:

- the right to a fair, public and independent trial
- freedom from laws which did not apply at the time of the 'offence'
- the right to an effective solution to a human rights issue
- freedom from discrimination.

The main types of judges and where they are found

Judges below High Court level are known as *inferior judges* and those above High Court level are known as *superior judges* (see diagram on p79 for inferior and superior judges). We will look at them in order of increasing power.

Inferior judges

District Judges (Magistrates' Courts)

This is a new type of judge born out of the **Access to Justice Act 1999**. They were previously known as *Stipendiary Magistrates*. They sit in the Magistrates' Courts and hear cases alone. Despite sitting in the Magistrates' Courts, District Judges (Magistrates' Courts) are fully legally qualified, with at least seven years' experience as a solicitor or barrister. They are also, unlike lay magistrates, full-time and fully paid.

Web activity

There are proposals from the Auld Report, which looked at the efficiency of the entire legal system, to produce a new type of court that will have these judges sitting with two lay magistrates to hear middle-ranking criminal cases. Seek out the Lord Chancellor's website for details of this ground-breaking report on www.open.gov.uk/lcd/. What are the key aims of this report? What resistance will these recommendations face, and from where?

District and Deputy District Judges

These judges hear civil cases in the County Courts, normally small claims cases. They are qualified solicitors or barristers with at least seven years' experience.

Recorders and Assistant Recorders

Recorders and Assistant Recorders are part-time judges who sit in the Crown Court. The rest of their time is spent practising as either solicitors or barristers. The job is on a fixed-term contract, normally of three years. At the end of this time either side can pull out. The job is used to see whether the person is suitable and able and wants to carry out the duties of a judge.

Circuit Judges

These judges listen to more complex civil cases that are heard in the County Courts. They may also be found in the Crown Court. They are either chosen from barristers and solicitors with at least ten years' experience or from existing Recorders and District Judges.

Superior judges

High Court Judges

High Court Judges are chosen from barristers or solicitors with at least ten years' experience or from those who have been Circuit Judges or academic lawyers. Applications can now be made by individuals since the **Court and Legal Services Act 1990**, but the Lord Chancellor still reserves the right to appoint who he thinks is the best candidate. High Court Judges sit in one of three courts: *The High Court* (Chancery, Queen's Bench and Family Divisions); *The Crown Court*, to listen to very serious cases; *The Divisional Courts*, to hear appeals.

Lord Justices of Appeal

These judges sit in the Court of Appeal and are selected from those who have had rights of audience in the High Court for ten years or from existing High Court Judges.

Lords of Appeal in Ordinary – the Law Lords

These judges sit in the House of Lords and are selected from those judges who have held senior judicial posts.

Web activity

Go to the Lord Chancellor's website and find more information about judges. Salaries are public information and are listed on this site: www.lcd.gov.uk. How do these salaries compare to those of senior barristers and solicitors?

Senior judiciary

This consists of:

- President of the Family Division of the High Court
- Vice Chancellor, who manages the Chancery Division
- Master of the Rolls, who is head of the Civil Division of the Court of Appeal
- Lord Chief Justice, who is head of the Criminal Division of the Court of Appeal
- The Lord Chancellor, who is a senior member of the Government and effectively in charge of the English courts system. This provides some problems about conflict of interest.

Web activity

Go to www.open.gov.uk/lcd/judicial/judgesfr.htm to find out the names of the current senior judiciary. It might be useful to know the key figures when reading news items about developments in the legal system.

5 Role of the Lord Chancellor

The Lord Chancellor acts as a link between three important parts of the legal-political system. He is:

- a member of the Cabinet, which means he plays a part at the heart of Government in a *political* capacity

- a member of the parliamentary process in the House of Lords, and therefore involved in the *legislative* process

- head of the Chancery Division of the High Court, so he plays an important *judicial* role.

The Lord Chancellor has a major part to play in the appointment of inferior and superior judges, and the Lord Chancellor's Department is a key Government institution. The Lord Chancellor is appointed by the Prime Minister and therefore often has strong personal and professional links with the heart of Government. The role is a strange one in a system that often has checks and balances to prevent the possibility of corruption and conflict of interest.

Group activity

1 There have been recent calls for the abolition of the job of Lord Chancellor. Do you agree, or is it important to have one person with an overview of the legal and political system?

2 Is the present system the most effective method of selecting judges? What other procedures might be possible in the selection of judges?

6 The Theory of Separation of Powers

Montesquieu was a French philosopher who believed that powers in a state should be separate. The power should be held in three areas so that no one area became too powerful:

- The *executive*, in other words the government that proposes the law

- The *legislative*, meaning the parliament that makes the law

- The *judicial*, that is, the judges, who see that the law is fairly enforced.

Our Lord Chancellor is present in all three of these areas. He is a member of Cabinet (the Government), he is a member of the House of Lords (the Parliament) and he is head of the Chancery Division of the High Court (the judiciary).

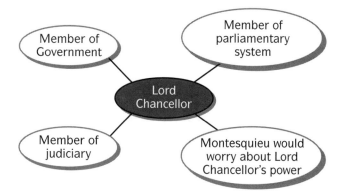

The role of the Lord Chancellor

Revision checklist

1 The Lord Chancellor plays an important part in all judicial appointments. Up to Circuit Judge level is by application and interviews; above this the Lord Chancellor approaches and suggests candidates.

2 Judges below High Court are called *inferior judges*. High Court Judges and above are called *superior judges*.

3 The Judicial Studies Board is responsible for the training of judges.

4 *Tenure* refers to job security. Dismissal of judges is difficult. Normally judges are persuaded to 'retire' rather than sacked.

5 Judges need to be independent and must resist pressure from Government, powerful companies, and the public and media.

6 The main roles of judges are: conducting trials, acting as legal experts, summing up and sentencing in criminal cases and giving the verdict and awarding damages in civil cases.

7 Judicial Review involves judges reviewing decisions made by lower courts and large public or private organizations.

8 The main types of judges are: District, Circuit, High Court and Appeal Judges.

9 The Lord Chancellor is a powerful political and legal figure who is seen in the government, the parliament and the judiciary.

10 The French philosopher Montesquieu thought is best to separate the three areas of power: the executive (government), the legislative (the parliament) and the judicial (the judges).

Quick revision questions

1 What changes did the Court and Legal Service Act bring to the appointment of judges?

2 Who appoints the most senior judges?

3 What is the role of the Judicial Studies Board?

4 How can judges be dismissed?

5 Where might pressure on judges come from?

6 What are the key duties of a judge?

7 What does the Judicial Review do?

8 What articles of the Human Rights Act most apply to the work of judges?

9 List the main types of judges in the English legal system.

10 Why would Montesquieu worry about the role of the Lord Chancellor?

Exam question

1 **a** How are judges selected for their posts? [20 marks]

    b What are the main criticisms of how judges are selected? [25 marks]

Exam answer guide

1 **a** Judges are selected in different ways depending on how high up the pecking order they are:

✓ Up to Circuit Judge level by advertisement, application and interview. The Lord Chancellor can still in theory appoint his own choice.

✓ Above Circuit Judge, the Lord Chancellor's Department collects information on suitable candidates and reports back to the Lord Chancellor. Candidates are approached and, if interested, appointed.

✓ For very senior judges, the Lord Chancellor suggests likely candidates to the Prime Minister. The suggestions are put in order of preference. The Prime Minister can choose to ignore the advice but normally follows the lead of the Lord Chancellor.

    b The process is not so bad for judges lower down the pile, but for more senior posts the process is secret and may be very unfair. Equal opportunities issues arise, as does the influence of the 'old boys' network'. The information collected by the Lord Chancellor's Department may be inaccurate and biased. Some say the influence and the power of the Lord Chancellor over appointments are too great.

UNIT 2

Barristers and solicitors

Key points

1 Training of barristers and solicitors
2 The work of barristers and solicitors
3 Supervisory roles of Bar Council and Law Society
4 Role of paralegals
5 Legal Services Ombudsman

Why do I need to know about barristers and solicitors?

Examination questions on this topic will expect you to be well aware of recent changes brought in by the Government. The **Court and Legal Services Act 1990** and the **Access to Justice Act 1999** are two of the most important. The Government is keen to open the legal profession to competition and sweep away outdated ways of working. It is vital that you are aware of the ongoing changes and employ them in your examination answers. Examiners need to see that students have a good grasp of current events as well as knowing the key points to the legal professional's job.

Access to Justice Act 1999

1 Training of barristers and solicitors

Barristers

There are approximately 10 000 barristers working in England and Wales. The organization responsible for the training and discipline of barristers is called the Bar Council. Unusually, the Bar Council also deals with complaints about barristers. There has been criticism of this system. As a result the Government is looking at a more independent complaints body. Much of this change has come via provisions made in the **Court and Legal Services Act 1990**.

There is a long training to be a barrister. Students follow one of two routes.

Route 1 to being a barrister

1   Take a law degree.

2   Next, do a one-year Bar Vocational Course (BVC). This is organized and monitored by the Bar Council and focuses on the skills needed when the law student becomes a barrister.

3   Join one of the four Inns of Court in London. This is an opportunity to meet, socialize with and make connections with more experienced barristers.

4   The next step is to be *called to the Bar*, which means the student is qualified as a barrister.

5   Before the newly qualified barrister can appear in court, however, they must find a place to become a pupil to an experienced barrister. This involves two separate six-month periods and is called *pupillage*. Normally the pupil barrister shadows a barrister for the first six months and for the next six months may represent clients in court.

Route 2 to being a barrister

1   Take a degree other than law.

2   Next, take the Common Professional Examination or the Postgraduate Diploma in Law. These are one-year conversion courses that cover key parts of a law degree.

3   Follow steps 2 to 5 from Route 1.

Web activity

Check university websites for law schools that provide the Bar Vocational Course. Find out in more detail the areas of law covered by the courses. What skills are developed when taking such a course?

Solicitors

Most people who need legal advice or legal work done start with the services of a solicitor. There are approximately 80 000 solicitors in the English and Welsh legal system.

Tough start!

Solicitors have the same type of training as barristers in the initial phase, but then go on to specialize.

1 Academic stage: a degree in law, or any other degree plus a Common Professional Examination/Postgraduate Diploma in Law.

2 A one-year course called the Legal Practice Course (LPC).

3 Two years of practical on-the-job training, including a Professional Skills Course which lasts 20 days.

4 Enrolment with the Law Society: the student is now a solicitor.

5 Ongoing training as they perform their duties as a solicitor.

Exam tip

Good time management in the exam is crucial if you want to answer all parts to each question well.

2 The work of barristers and solicitors

The work of barristers

You may have seen a Crown Court in action, or barristers at work in TV programmes such as *Kavanagh QC* and *Judge John Deed*. Their main duties are:

● acting as advocates for clients in the Crown Court

● preparing 'opinion' for clients, which means giving their view on legal issues – they are often asked whether a case is worth pursuing

● preparing pre-trial papers to make sure that the case they are working on is processed as efficiently as possible.

Once they qualify, barristers are normally self-employed. They are not allowed to form partnerships. They work together with other barristers in a workplace called *chambers*. The barristers share the building, a clerk and the other running expenses of the building. The clerk arranges the business of the chambers, allocates the cases and often negotiates the fees charged for work.

Obstacles for newly qualified barristers

The financial realities of a barrister's life can cause problems. Many students leave undergraduate degree courses with considerable debt. Student barristers have to cope with the added burden of the Bar Vocational Course and a year as a pupil.

For those without wealthy backgrounds, the early days can be a real struggle. Fees are normally a long time in coming to the newly established barrister. The effect of this is that many new members of the profession leave before they become established.

Group activity

The tremendous financial commitments involved in the training of barristers often prove impossible for many young barristers and their families to cope with. How might the legal profession and their clients lose out from such a state of affairs?

Promotion of barristers

Once a barrister has been working for ten years they can apply to become a Queen's Counsel, known as a QC. This is an honorary title much cherished by barristers. It is awarded by the Lord Chancellor to the best of the junior barristers in the country. All barristers are called Junior Barristers until made Queen's Counsel.

There are many advantages to being a QC. Social status is enhanced, and in their professional role QCs can charge more for their work and receive more interesting and important cases.

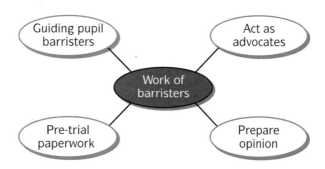

The work of barristers

The QC

Quick questions

What are the two main routes to becoming a barrister?

The final stage in the life of a barrister may be elevation to the judiciary. Although judges are well paid, some barristers may have to take a pay cut to become a judge. The status is usually enough of a lure.

The work of solicitors

Solicitors work in a number of areas, including:

- acting as advocates in the Magistrates' Courts
- drawing up and processing last wills and testaments
- divorce proceedings
- issues concerning tax
- the production of commercial contracts.

A solicitor may work as part of a solicitors' practice or eventually run their own business. About 15 per cent of solicitors seek employment outside the private sector, working instead with local authorities, the Crown Prosecution Service, Government departments, etc.

Index card revision

Using index cards, note the key points on the training, work and promotion of barristers.

The work of solicitors is varied and although there used to be very strict separation between what solicitors and barristers do in the legal world, this is gradually breaking down. **The Court and Legal Services Act 1990** has been partly responsible for these fundamental changes. A solicitor needs a Certificate of Advocacy to work in the Crown Court and above.

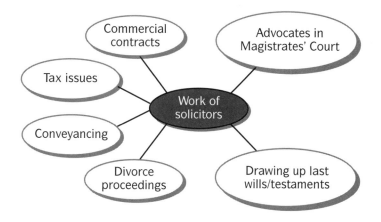

The work of solicitors

Promotion of solicitors

Increasingly, solicitors may be seen in higher courts representing clients. This was formerly the area barristers specialized in, but since the passing of the **Court and Legal Services Act 1990**, solicitors have been given more opportunities for their skills. It is still to be seen whether solicitors with the Certificate of Advocacy get the same opportunities for work in the judiciary.

Legal case: *Hall v Simons (2000)*

This case clarified the legal position of solicitors who were sued by their clients. Their immunity from prosecution seems to have been lifted in all areas. Prior to this, solicitors and barristers could not be sued for their work as advocates since it was felt that clients might blame the skills of the lawyer rather than accept that the case might have been very difficult to win by anyone.

Other changes to the world of solicitors and barristers

In addition to the many changes to the professions pushed through by the Government, other developments are also taking place.

Competition from supermarket locations

Competition to more traditional law practices may soon come from firms who hope to take the law to the shopper. Law outlets are being planned for shopping centres and other High Street and community locations where potential customers may be found.

Telephone advice 0898 style

Some solicitors operate premium-rate telephone lines that are advertised in local newspapers. No demand for payment is made, apart from an inflated phone bill. Clearly this is an effective way to start a relationship with a potential client.

An alternative?

Internet advice

In the United States, Internet law advice is on the increase, and it is probably only a matter of time before it develops in the United Kingdom. It may be difficult to hold the adviser to account if things go wrong, but it may be cheaper for straightforward legal tips.

Claims direct

The 'no win no fee' system introduced as the result of changes to the Legal Aid scheme has produced a number of companies who drum up business for solicitors' firms using large-scale TV promotions and by handing out leaflets in the High Street.

3 Supervisory roles of Bar Council and Law Society

The Bar Council oversees the training, work and discipline of barristers. It is a powerful, self-regulating organization, which makes up its own rules and is very defensive of its members. Change is something it prefers to ignore.

Web activity

Check out the barristers' trade union, the Bar Council, at its website: www.barcouncil.org.uk. What services does it offer barristers? What are the key issues the Bar Council is struggling with at the moment?

Solicitors also have a professional body. It is called the Law Society. It supports solicitors, but also uses a disciplinary procedure if there are any complaints made by the public against a solicitor. It oversees training and provides a number of support services. The Law Society, like the Bar Council, is coming under pressure for change and modernization.

Web activity

Find the Law Society's website at www.lawsociety.org.uk. Investigate the aims of the Law Society and the services it offers to its members. What current issues is it attempting to deal with?

4 Role of paralegals

Paralegals work in the world of law, but in a support role to solicitors and barristers. There is a Paralegal Association which represents their interests, but they are not as firmly established or as well known as the bigger group – legal executives, who are represented by their own professional body, the Institute of Legal Executives (ILEX).

Legal executives

Legal executives are the biggest and most important group of non-professional but legally qualified workers. They work alongside barristers or solicitors. There are around 23 000 legal executives.

Training of legal executives

Legal executives work while they train. If they join straight from school they can expect to earn £8–9000 per year. After they are fully qualified they can expect to earn £20–24 000 per year.

They have to take courses and examinations organized by their professional body, the Institute of Legal Executives (ILEX). The training is a combination of self-study, evening courses and day-release. The employer often helps with the cost of the course.

There are three main steps to becoming a fully qualified legal executive.

1 Student: a series of courses covering areas encountered in the legal profession, i.e. family law, civil disputes, criminal cases and conveyancing.

2 Membership: students apply for enrolment after completing parts 1 and 2 of their membership qualification.

3 Fellowship: for full admission, candidates must be at least 25 years old and have five years' experience in a legal office.

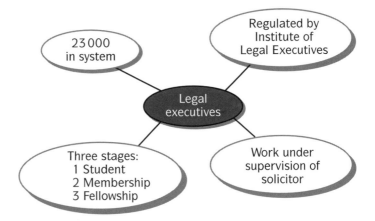

Legal executives

Work of legal executives

The day-to-day work of a legal executive is very similar to that of a solicitor. Legal executives can often find themselves in the front line when dealing with clients. They go to court to support solicitors and may be asked to attend police stations to gather information from clients who are being held in custody. Legal executives always work under the supervision of a solicitor. They have a very flexible career and training structure which can lead to fully qualified legal status as a solicitor.

Web activity

Explore the Institute of Legal Executives website at www.ilex.org.uk. Gather further information about the career routes open to members of ILEX and the personal qualities that they are expected to possess.

5 Legal Services Ombudsman

The Legal Services Ombudsman (LSO) investigates the way complaints about either barristers or solicitors are dealt with. The LSO system is not designed as an appeal process. If it is believed, however, that the original complaint was not dealt with properly, the LSO will ask the Bar Council or Law Society to review the matter. The LSO is keen to see that the disciplinary body arrived at a decision that was reasonable.

The Legal Services Ombudsman was established as part of the **Court and Legal Services Act 1990**. The full power of the ombudsman has yet to be felt. The Government hopes that self-regulation will eventually work, but it is felt by many that time is running out for the current disciplinary procedures.

Web activity

Go to the website for the Legal Services Ombudsman at www.olso.org and find out why this service exists. Why is the Government keen to use such a body?

Revision checklist

1 There are approximately 10 000 barristers in the English legal system who are supported, trained and disciplined by their association, the Bar Council.

2 Training for barristers includes: law degree (or Common Professional Examination post graduate diploma in law), Bar Vocational Course, and one year as a pupil barrister.

3 There are approximately 80 000 solicitors in the English legal system who are supported, trained and disciplined by their association, the Law Society.

4 Training for solicitors includes: degree in law (or Common Professional Examination/Postgraduate Diploma in Law), Legal Practice Course, two years of on-the-job training (including 20-day Professional Skills Course).

5 Work of barristers involves: acting as advocates, normally in the Crown Court; preparing opinions for clients; and pre-trial paperwork.

6 After ten years, barristers may become Queen's Counsel, which is an honorary title signifying excellence, awarded by the Lord Chancellor.

7 Work of solicitors involves: acting as advocate, normally in the Magistrates' Court, working on last wills and testaments and probate, divorce proceedings and commercial work, such as tax and contracts.

8 Solicitors may act as advocates in the higher courts if they possess a Certificate of Advocacy.

9 Paralegals work alongside solicitors and barristers. The biggest branch is legal executives.

10 The Legal Services Ombudsman investigates cases of poor service on behalf of the public.

Revision questions

1 Outline the routes to becoming a barrister.

2 Outline the routes to becoming a solicitor.

3 What are the key functions of a barrister?

4 What are the key functions of a solicitor?

5 What is a Queen's Counsel?

6 Name a key aim of the **Court and Legal Services Act 1990**.

7 What does the Bar Council do?

8 What does the Law Society do?

9 What are the main duties of legal executives?

10 Which Act of Parliament created the Legal Services Ombudsman?

Exam question

1 a Outline the main training stages of solicitors and barristers. [20 marks]
   b What are the criticisms of the present system of training? [25 marks]

Exam answer guide

1 a The main training stages are:
   ✓ Academic – the degree course
   ✓ Vocational – the Bar Vocational Course (BVC) or the Legal Practice Course (LPC)
   ✓ Professional – two-year training contract for solicitors and the pupillage for a barrister.
   Outline in brief what each of these stages consists of.

   b Criticisms are about equal opportunities and access for the less well-off.
   ✓ BVC is very expensive
   ✓ Little financial support for a pupil barrister
   ✓ Training contracts very difficult to get; it might be useful if they already know someone in the system
   ✓ Training can take many years, which means huge debts for ordinary students.
   The overall result may be a very elitist legal profession. Barristers may not understand or be able to communicate effectively with the clients they hope to serve. Good-quality potential barrister candidates who do not have the necessary financial background may be lost.

Crown Prosecution Service

Key points

1 The role of the Crown Prosecution Service
2 Personnel
3 Director of Public Prosecutions

Why do I need to know about the Crown Prosecution Service?

Examination questions will expect you to know about the key part the Crown Prosecution Service (CPS) plays in tying together the investigators of crime and the court process. The Crown Prosecution Service plays a vital part in the whole chain of events from police station to court, and then on to sentence or release. You need to know how the chain links together and the role the CPS plays. You also need to know how the CPS decides on which cases to pursue, and also how it works with other parts of the Criminal Justice System. See also Module 1 Unit 4: Police powers, Unit 5: Criminal courts, and Unit 4 in this module: Lay magistrates.

Crown Prosecution Service

1 The role of the Crown Prosecution Service

The Crown Prosecution Service (CPS) was set up in 1985 by the **Prosecution of Offences Act**. Its main function is the prosecution of alleged offenders in England and Wales. This used to be the job of the police, but it was felt that an independent and specialized body would accomplish the task more effectively and give greater consistency across the Criminal Justice System. The police still play an important role by submitting the evidence they have collected to the CPS.

The role of the CPS can be split into five key areas which are:

- advising the police on possible prosecution of offenders
- reviewing prosecutions started by the police to ensure all charges are correct and details are in order
- preparing cases for prosecution by the court
- prosecuting cases at the Magistrates' Court and instructing lawyers for cases to be heard in the Crown Court and above
- working with other groups to improve the efficiency of the criminal justice system.

Prosecution of cases

The decision to prosecute a case depends on two key tests, both of which must be passed if a prosecution is to proceed.

1 Is there enough evidence?

- The evidence must be allowed by the rules of the court, i.e. admissible.
- The evidence must be reliable.
- The evidence must be substantial so that there is a 'reasonable prospect' of a successful prosecution.

Work of the CPS

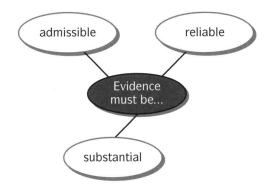

Is there enough evidence?

2 Is it in the public interest?

- – Was a weapon used against the victim?
- – Was the motive for the offence based on some type of discrimination?
- – Was a police officer or other public servant, such as a nurse or a firefighter, involved as a victim?
- – Was the defendant in a position of trust or responsibility?

There are some factors which might encourage the CPS not to press for a prosecution.

- There is likely to be only a token punishment.
- A sentence is already being served for an offence and a new conviction would seem unwarranted.
- The offence was the result of a mistake or misjudgement.
- The harm caused to the victim was relatively minor.
- There has been a long delay.

The CPS works with a Code of Practice to ensure that all parties involved in the process of prosecution are aware of the stages involved and the safeguards in place.

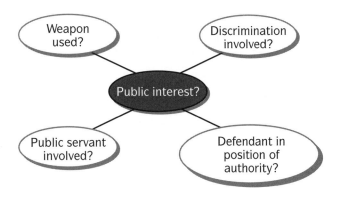

Is it in the public interest?

One major criticism that has been made of the CPS is that it does not follow enough cases through to prosecution. Victims and victims' families clearly have strong views on the prosecution of offenders, but the CPS must apply its evidence and public interest tests. The most famous example where this has caused a major upset was in the Stephen Lawrence case. This young black man was murdered in a racist attack, but the CPS felt there was insufficient evidence to prosecute. The family of Stephen Lawrence took out a private prosecution, but the case was thrown out of court by the judge for insufficient evidence.

Legal case: *R v Field (2001)*

Clearly the CPS may still prosecute a very serious crime even if there has been a very long time delay. A case involving the tragic murder of a number of young children in the 1970s was successfully completed with a guilty verdict in November 2001. The murderer was convicted using DNA sampling techniques. When he was arrested for drunk driving he gave the police a sample which matched with samples taken at the murder scene 30 years earlier.

Presentation of the case

If it is decided that there is enough evidence for the case to proceed and that it is in the public interest, then the case is heard in the Magistrates' Court. It is prosecuted by a CPS lawyer who is under obligation to present the case fairly and reveal all relevant information. If the case is a serious one it is passed up to the Crown Court. These indictable offences are heard by barristers hired (instructed) by the CPS.

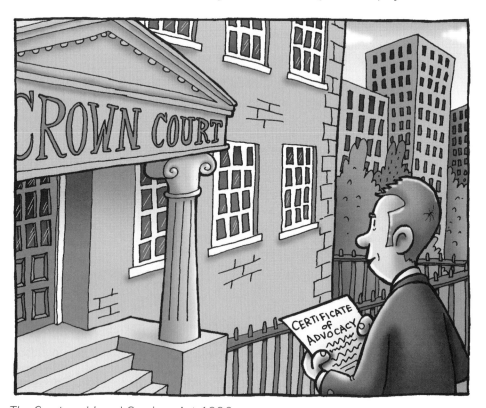

The Court and Legal Services Act 1990

The CPS and the police

The police and the CPS must work effectively together if they are to secure fair and effective convictions. When the CPS was founded, it acted as a national service from a central office. It now has 42 regional offices, and these are able to work with the 42 police forces on a local level to increase effectiveness and save taxpayers' money. A number of joint schemes have improved communication. For example, CPS lawyers work in police stations advising on cases and ensuring that standards are uniform across the country. Also, task forces containing police and CPS members identify weaknesses in the system and improve the management of the service. The bureaucracy of the service is constantly monitored to reduce unnecessary paperwork.

The CPS and the Probation Service

Since 1992 the CPS has worked closely with the Probation Service in helping with pre-sentence reports. The Probation Service has a duty to assess the nature of offences committed by the defendant, and this is where the expertise of the CPS is useful.

2 Personnel

The CPS has its own advocates working in the Magistrates' Courts. They prepare the evidence collected by the police and present the case in court. Barristers instructed by the CPS deal with cases in the Crown Court. The **Court and Legal Services Act 1990** and the **Access to Justice Act 1999** are attempting to see solicitors hearing cases in the higher courts. It may be possible in the future to see many more directly employed solicitors prosecuting cases in the Crown Court.

In addition to prosecutors in the Magistrates' Court, a Chief Crown Prosecutor heads each of the 42 regional offices of the CPS and is responsible for liaison with the police and for the work of the prosecutors dealing with cases.

3 Director of Public Prosecutions

The Director of Public Prosecutions (DPP) is head of the Crown Prosecution Service. The post of DPP has been around for a very long time and covers more than just the work of the CPS. The expansion of the CPS has, of course, expanded the role and power of the DPP in the Criminal Justice System. The DPP may get personally involved in very serious or important cases that go through the CPS.

Revision checklist

1 The Crown Prosecution Service (CPS) was established in 1985 to prosecute criminal cases.

2 Its main functions are: advising the police, reviewing cases started by the police, preparing cases for prosecution, prosecuting offenders at the Magistrates' Court, hiring lawyers to prosecute offenders in the Crown Court, and working with other groups to improve the efficiency of the Criminal Justice System.

3 Prosecution proceeds if the CPS decides there is enough evidence and it is in the public interest.

4 Evidence must be: admissible, reliable, and substantial.

5 Prosecution is in the public interest if: weapon used, discrimination involved, public servant involved, defendant in position of authority.

6 Prosecution is unlikely if: punishment is likely to be only token punishment, sentence already being served and prosecution is not necessary, offence result of a mistake, harm caused is minor or there has been a long delay.

7 CPS has been criticized for dropping too many cases.

8 CPS has 42 local offices which work closely with the 42 police forces.

9 CPS has its own personnel prosecuting offences in the Magistrates' Courts; **Access to Justice Act 1999** may see more CPS people in higher courts.

10 The Director of Public Prosecutions is head of the CPS and gets personally involved in very important cases.

Quick revision questions

1 What are the five key duties of the CPS?

2 When was the CPS formed?

3 Who prosecuted cases before the CPS?

4 What two criteria are used to decide whether to continue with a case?

5 Name three circumstances that would encourage the CPS to prosecute.

6 Name three circumstances that would reduce the possibility of a prosecution by the CPS.

7 What types of lawyers are employed by the CPS?

8 What has been the major criticism of the CPS?

9 What is the relationship between the police and the CPS?

10 What does the Director of Public Prosecutions do?

1 a Outline the work of the Crown Prosecution Service. [20 marks]

   b Why is it important to have an independent service to prosecute cases? [25 marks]

Exam answer guide

1 a The Crown Prosecution Service has the following functions:

✓ Advising the police

✓ Reviewing prosecutions

✓ The preparation of cases for prosecution

✓ Prosecuting cases at the Magistrates' Court

✓ Instructing lawyers for cases to be heard in the Crown Court and above

✓ Working with other groups to improve the efficiency of the Criminal Justice System.

   b An independent service is important because:

✓ It separates investigators from prosecutors

✓ It provides more professional service

✓ It takes pressure off police

✓ Two systems working closely together keep a check on each other.

Prosecution of cases is controversial. Some cases cause public unhappiness because they are not prosecuted and some because they are. An independent service may be able to withstand the heat and make more impartial decisions. A useful case to quote is that of Stephen Lawrence.

Lay magistrates

Key points

1 Appointment of magistrates
2 Social background
3 Training
4 Role of lay magistrates
5 Evaluation and criticism
6 Role of the Magistrate's Clerk

Why do I need to know about lay magistrates?

You will need to give answers that demonstrate an understanding of how magistrates are selected and appointed. You will need to know what magistrates' duties are and what proposals for reform are currently under review. You will need to identify strengths and weaknesses in the current system and comment on suggested improvements. The Auld Report is essential reading in this area.

The magistrates

This unit explores not only the present structure but also some of the key proposals affecting magistrates. If you can demonstrate insights into current legal debates you will impress examiners.

1 Appointment of magistrates

Anyone between the ages of 21 and 60 may be considered as a candidate to be a magistrate. In reality, however, few people under the age of 27 are called for interview. A local Advisory Committee considers applications, interviews candidates and puts forward suitable names to the Lord Chancellor's Department. It is hoped that the candidates elected as lay magistrates by the Lord Chancellor will represent a broad range of the local community.

Magistrates can serve until 70 years old, but then they must retire. They can be removed for incompetence or if they gain a criminal conviction. This happens to about ten magistrates a year. This is a very small number considering there are 30 000 magistrates in the system.

The Lord Chancellor's Department has listed some important qualities that it believes magistrates should have. A magistrate must:

- be of good character
- have personal integrity
- have sound common sense
- have the ability to weigh up evidence and reach a conclusion
- be able to work as a member of a team
- be firm yet compassionate.

Web activity

The Lord Chancellor's Department is a key Government department that coordinates and administers the court system. Visit the site at www.open.gov.uk/lcd/ and make a list of the key functions of the department.

Key qualities for magistrates

Glossary

An **undischarged bankrupt** is a person who is unable to meet his or her debts and is under the control of a court. The person may choose to declare themselves bankrupt or may be taken to court by a person who is owed money.

Magistrates must live within fifteen miles of the Court and have lived in the locality for a minimum of one year. Magistrates must have a good local knowledge of the area and the people they are dealing with.

Certain people are not allowed to become magistrates. They include.

- anyone not of good character and standing
- undischarged bankrupts
- members of the armed forces
- members of the police
- traffic wardens
- close relatives of someone on the same bench
- anyone who cannot carry out the duties because of a disability.

Glossary

Social background refers to whether the person is working class, middle class or upper class.

2 Social background

There has been some criticism of the lack of balance between different **social backgrounds** among magistrates. Magistrates are more often than not middle-class, middle-aged professionals. Defendants often have socially and economically underprivileged backgrounds. Some argue that magistrates may not fully understand these issues of deprivation.

Exam tip

Answer only the question on the paper. Do not simply write everything you know about magistrates.

The six key qualities

Index card revision

Summarize the points relating to selection and training of lay magistrates.

Latest figures from the Magistrates' Association show a good gender mix and a reasonable number of people from ethnic minority backgrounds. The political and social mix is, however, typically Conservative, middle-class and middle-aged. There are several reasons for this.

● Working people find it difficult to get time off work even though the **Employment Act 1996** obliges employers to allow this.

● Owners of businesses and more senior employees may be able to arrange time off work more easily.

● Retired people or those at home may have more time on their hands.

● Conservative supporters may be more interested in law and order issues.

● Younger workers may be trying to get a career going and having families, so do not have the time.

● Middle-class people may have more confidence in dealing with the application and interview process that goes with being a magistrate.

Group activity

How should the Lord Chancellor's Department tackle the lack of young and working-class magistrates?

3 Training

Training is now a key area of concern for the Lord Chancellor's Department. Inconsistent verdicts and sentences have led to concerns about support and training given to magistrates. Magistrates are given some training before they listen to and decide on cases. They now continue to receive training throughout their service. A recent scheme, known as Magistrates' New Training Initiative (MNTI), has developed a mentor-based process. It is hoped that MNTI will provide support for new magistrates. MNTI aims to help magistrates:

● understand basic law and procedure

● develop skills in making fair but firm judgments

● develop team-working skills.

Did you know?

The **Human Rights Act 1998** was actually introduced in October 2000. It protects British citizens and allows them to use British courts for human rights issues.

Recent events such as the **Human Rights Act 1998** and the publication of the far-reaching Stephen Lawrence Enquiry Report have focused attention once again on the importance of high-quality training for those working in the magistrates' system.

All the training undertaken by magistrates is in their own time, in the evenings and at weekends. The extra training required of magistrates when the Human Rights Act came into force led many magistrates to resign.

4 Role of lay magistrates

The English legal system relies heavily on **lay** people in the administration of justice. They are felt to bring the system 'down to earth' and allow the 'ordinary person' an opportunity to participate in the machinery of justice.

A crucial part played by lay people is when they undertake the duties of a lay magistrate. Lay magistrates are part-time judges who hear minor criminal cases at the local Magistrates' Court. Lay magistrates are not legally qualified. They do, however, receive training to help them with their duties. There are about 30 000 lay magistrates in the English legal system. They listen to approximately 98 per cent of all criminal cases and refer the rest to higher courts.

Duties of magistrates

Lay magistrates normally spend between 26 and 35 half-days per year hearing cases in the Magistrates' Court. Lay magistrates are unpaid except for expenses such as travel and subsistence. They sit in twos and threes on **the bench**. Their chief duties are:

● Dealing with *summary offences*. These are minor offences which can only be heard in the Magistrates' Court. They include criminal damage cases worth less than £5000 and the majority of minor driving offences.

● Dealing with '*either way' offences/triable 'either way' offences*. These are cases which can be heard in the Magistrates' or the Crown Court. If agreement is reached, the magistrate will hear the case. These offences are often crimes like theft or burglary.

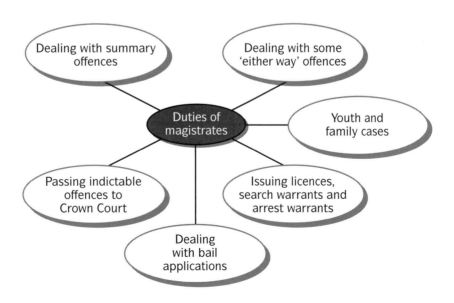

The duties of magistrates

- Passing *indictable cases* to higher courts. These are the most serious cases, which are beyond the sentencing powers of the Magistrates' Court. They include cases such as murder, rape and grievous bodily harm.

- Deciding bail conditions for defendants and the issuing of arrest warrants.

- Hearing youth and family cases in special separate courts. Magistrates receive additional training for these important areas of their work.

- Granting licences for the sale of alcohol and the staging of entertainment events.

In addition to lay people, the Magistrates' Courts also use District Judges (Magistrates' Court). These judges are legally qualified and are paid a salary. There are only about a hundred of these professional magistrates in the country, half of whom sit in London courts. They hear more complex and difficult cases. They used to be called *Stipendiary Magistrates*.

Magistrates are entitled to time off work to perform their duties, although some employers are not always supportive. Loss of earnings allowances are paid if the magistrate loses money from carrying out their job as a magistrate.

Web activity

Access the Magistrates' Association website at www.magistrates-association.org.uk and identify quotes from employers on the value they attach to having magistrates in their workplace.

1 What skills do you think magistrates might develop as the result of the work in court?

2 How might this be used in other areas of their life?

Powers of magistrates

When magistrates hear a summary offence they have the following powers at their disposal:

- imprisonment of the convicted defendant for up to six months

- suspended sentence of imprisonment

- a fine of £5000

- an order to pay compensation up to a maximum figure of £5000

- probation order

- community service order

- conditional discharge

- absolute discharge

- hospital order

- drug abstinence order

- drug treatment order

- curfew order.

Magistrates refer more serious cases, which are beyond their **sentencing powers**, upwards to the Crown Court. This is known as a *committal*.

5 Evaluation and criticism

Strengths of the magistrates system

There are clear advantages to both the Government and the public of using the present system of lay magistrates. The present system:

- is cheap and fairly quick
- allows local participation, which gives public faith in the system
- has an experienced, qualified clerk guiding the proceedings
- is covered by the **Human Rights Act 1998**, which now ensures fuller explanations for decisions
- has improved training, allowing better quality of trials and decisions.

Weaknesses of the magistrates system

There are, however, some problems with the present system.

- Magistrates tend to be from one social group, the middle class.
- Sentencing can vary considerably from one court to another.
- Quantity of work means quality may get worse.
- Magistrates are much more likely to convict.
- Cases are not heard in as much detail compared to in the Crown Court.

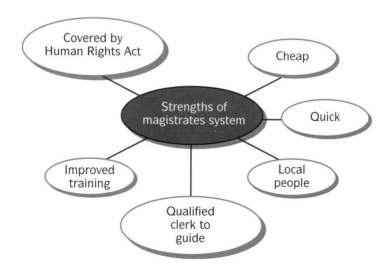

The magistrates system has its strengths

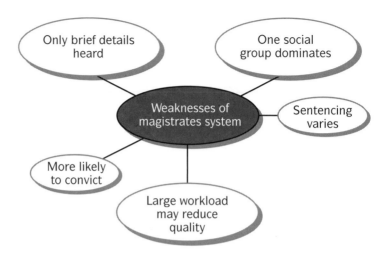

The system also has weaknesses

Reform of the magistrates system

There are a number of pressures and developments that have led to proposals for reform of the system.

Cost

Active consideration has already been given to reducing the rights to a jury trial in some circumstances and trying the defendant at the Magistrates' Court. This would considerably reduce the costs involved in hearing cases at the Crown Court. This may mean increasing the present sentencing powers of the magistrates. Human rights groups, members of the general public and some MPs have doubts about this development.

The Human Rights Act 1998

The Human Rights Act 1998 promises a fair hearing for all defendants, with an effective appeals procedure. Before the passing of the Act magistrates were not forced to give reasons for their verdicts or their sentencing. This **accountability** should improve the quality of decision-making and sentencing.

Information technology

The Government is keen to make the justice system as cost-effective and as speedy as possible. One possible path is the use of more information technology in the courts. It is unlikely that we will see video-phone trials, but a great deal of the paperwork might be handled more effectively by computer systems.

Greater use of qualified and paid magistrates

There are only approximately one hundred District Judges (previously known as Stipendiary Magistrates). Problems with the decisions of some Magistrates' Courts, particularly in the area of dubious sentencing, have led to some pressure for more full-time professional magistrates. Cost is obviously an obstacle here.

Glossary

Accountability means being responsible to a body or person outside of yourself. It means that you have to answer for your decisions.

Fully qualified paid magistrates could pose some problems

Group activity

The Metropolitan Police Commissioner has recently called for all-night courts after seeing them in operation in New York City. Present courts seem to be based around the working patterns of those involved in the administration of the system rather than around victims and defendants. Defendants and victims may want to get the case heard and out of the way sooner rather than later. Some believe, however, that late hours will cause disruption amongst solicitors, the prison service and court staff.

1 Outline the advantages and disadvantages to the various groups involved in the court system.

2 Evaluate the effectiveness of such a system in the UK.

The Auld Report

Sir Robin Auld's Report (October 2001) makes 300 recommendations for changes and improvements to the courts system. Some will affect the Magistrates' Courts:

● Some cases will be transferred from the Crown Court to the Magistrates' Court. This means a reduction in the defendant's right to choose where the case is heard.

Barrister's nightmare

- A new court containing two magistrates and one District Judge will be created to hear middle-ranking offences.
- Some cases now heard by magistrates, such as failure to pay a TV licence, will now be processed by post. The case will never come in front of a court.

6 Role of the Magistrates' Clerk

As magistrates are not legally qualified, the Magistrates' Clerk assists. Magistrates' Clerks are there to give guidance on matters of law, court procedure and practice. The Magistrates' Clerk often has a diploma in magisterial law. The magistrates, rather than the clerk, are solely responsible for deciding the facts of the case and the sentencing of the defendant.

Revision checklist

1 People between 27 and 60 are normally considered as magistrates.

2 Magistrates can serve until they are 70 unless removed by the Lord Chancellor for misbehaviour or criminal conviction. About ten per year are removed.

3 The Lord Chancellor has listed six key qualities magistrates must have: good character, personal integrity, common sense, ability to make decisions, team player and compassion with firmness.

4 Certain people are not allowed to become magistrates: bad characters, members of the armed forces, police, traffic wardens, relatives of magistrates in the same court, anyone who cannot carry out duties because of a disability.

5 Social background has been criticized for being too middle-class and Conservative.

6 Training now seen as a key area for magistrates; a new scheme is known as MINTI.

7 Magistrates hear minor cases called summary cases and some triable either way cases in the Magistrates' Court.

8 Magistrates can imprison for up to six months or fine up to £5000 per offence.

9 Strengths of the magistrates: cheap, local participation, qualified Magistrates' Clerk, **Human Rights Act 1998** used, improved training.

10 Weaknesses of the magistrates: One social group dominates, sentencing can vary, quantity of work may reduce quality, magistrates more likely to convict, cases not heard in detail.

Quick revision questions

1 What are the normal ages of appointment and retirement for magistrates?

2 What are the six key qualities the Lord Chancellor wants in a magistrate?

3 Who cannot become a magistrate?

4 Which social group dominates the magistracy?

5 Give reasons why younger working-class people do not apply.

6 What are the aims of training for magistrates?

7 What are the key jobs of a magistrate?

8 What powers do magistrates have?

9 What are the key strengths of the present system of magistrates?

10 What are the key weaknesses of the present system of magistrates?

Exam question

1 a What do lay magistrates do? [20 marks]

  b Do you think magistrates can deliver sound judgments? [25 marks]

Exam answer guide

1 a Magistrates:
- ✓ Hear minor criminal cases (summary cases)
- ✓ Hear either way (medium serious) criminal cases
- ✓ Commit more serious criminal cases (indictable), to the Crown Court
- ✓ Listen to appeals from the magistrates in the Crown Court accompanied by a Crown Court judge.
- ✓ Deal with bail applications, search warrants and warrants for arrest.

  b Magistrates can deliver sound judgments because:
- ✓ They are thoroughly interviewed and carefully selected
- ✓ They have to have the six key qualities that the Lord Chancellor wants
- ✓ They receive training and have a mentor who gives guidance
- ✓ They have a Magistrates' Clerk to help with the law
- ✓ There is an appeal procedure if it all goes wrong.

However, the following obstacles may hinder sound judgments:
- ✓ They are not legally qualified
- ✓ They do seem to come from one particular background
- ✓ They are more likely to convict than in the Crown Court
- ✓ Conviction rates can widely vary from one bench to another.

Look at both positions and *give your own view*.

Juries

Key points

1 Qualifications of jurors
2 Selection of jury panels
3 Role in criminal and in civil cases
4 Evaluation and criticism of the jury system
5 Alternatives to jury trial

Why do I need to know about juries?

The second way in which an ordinary person can play a part in the legal system is by being a member of a jury. Questions in exams will ask you about the method of selection of juries, who can and who cannot serve and how far jurors are representative of the population. The Auld Report promises changes to the present system, and the Government is keen to see a reduction in the number of expensive jury trials. You will need to have an opinion on this important issue. Link this unit with Module 1 Unit 5, Criminal courts.

The jury

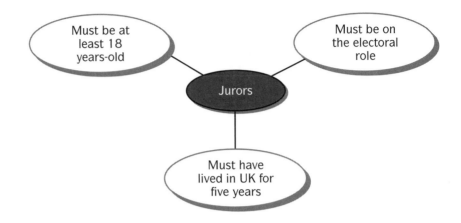

Jurors

1 Qualifications of jurors

There are some basic requirements that need to be met before a citizen is considered as a member of a jury. They must:

- be listed on the electoral role

- be at least 18 years-old

- have lived in the UK for five years since they were thirteen years old.

People on the electoral role aged between 65 and 70 do not have to serve if they do not want to. People over 70 are not selected for jury service.

Some people, on the other hand, are disqualified because of their jobs or personal circumstances. They include:

- police officers and traffic wardens

- barristers and solicitors

- people with mental illnesses

- people who have been in prison or have received a **suspended prison sentence** within the last ten years.

Glossary

Suspended sentence: The defendant is not put in prison unless they commit another crime within a certain period of time.

---

2 Selection of jury panels

Method of selection

The jury is selected at random from the electoral register to provide a cross-section of the population. There is further selection at the court itself, using cards to choose twelve jurors at random from a pool of possible jury members.

Excusal

Some people do not have serve if they do not wish to. It is their right to refuse.

- MPs do not have to serve, but can if they wish.

- Doctors do not have to serve as their job is important to others.

- Members of the armed forces would find it almost impossible to arrange, so they are excused.

- People who have served within the last two years have done their duty and are excused from jury service if they choose to be.

Discretion of judge

The judge will decide on these individual cases whether someone should serve or not. They may be asked to serve at a later date.

- Parents with young children may find it difficult to serve as jurors.

- People who have pre-booked holidays may be excused by the judge.

- Students with examinations may be excused to serve at a later date.

Group activity

Do you think that the present system with so many exemptions is the best way to select a jury? Some have called for a system that has no exemptions. Would this give better results? Look again at the various groups who are exempt, disqualified and excused.

Discretion of the judge

Exam tip

Examination
questions about lay
people will expect
you to consider not
only jurors but also
magistrates in your
answers.

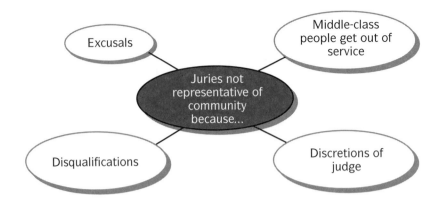

Why juries are not representative of the community

3 Role in criminal and in civil cases

The duties of a jury member in criminal cases

A jury must listen to the more serious cases dealt with by the criminal justice
system. A jury member is there to make decisions on the evidence that is put in
front of them and decide whether the defendant is guilty or not guilty.

Juries take part in criminal cases in the Crown Court and sometimes in civil cases
in the County Court and High Court. The defence and prosecution will attempt to
convince the jury members that their version of what happened is the truth. The
jury will listen to witnesses called by the defence and the prosecution. When the
courtroom evidence has been heard, they will withdraw to discuss the case and
reach a verdict.

Criminal cases

These cases are heard in the Crown Court when a defendant pleads not guilty.
The jury decides whether the defendant is guilty or not guilty, whilst the judge
oversees the legal aspects of the case. A jury must return a unanimous verdict if
it can, but if it cannot a majority verdict of 11–1 or 10–2 will be accepted,
provided the jury discusses the case for at least two hours and ten minutes. The
ten minutes is to cover travelling time between jury box and jury room. This
subject is also discussed in Module 1 Unit 5.

The duties of a jury in civil cases

A jury, which is used very rarely in these cases, hears actions involving fraud,
defamation of character, false imprisonment and malicious prosecution. In other
words, the only civil cases allowed to have a jury are ones where a person's
reputation and good name are at risk. The jury's task is to decide which side has
won the case and how much should be paid in damages. When a case is heard in
the County Court, a jury of **eight** is used. The High Court requires **twelve**.

Juries differ in size

Group activity

Bruce Grobbelaar, the famous goalkeeper, was subject to a civil case involving corruption and match-fixing. After the jury had decided the outcome, the judge dismissed the jury's verdict as 'perverse' and refused to accept it. He ordered a retrial.

1 Do you judge was right to do so if he felt strongly about the issue?

2 Should this be allowed to happen in criminal cases also?

4 Evaluation and criticism of the jury system

The jury system has been around for hundreds of years in one form or another. There are both advantages and disadvantages to it.

Strengths of the jury system

- The general public are very keen to maintain trial by jury. Ordinary people have a part to play in the system.

- Professionals have to make sure that jurors who are not legally qualified understand the proceedings. Thus the system is kept accessible to all.

- The use of ordinary people brings the system down to earth.

- A group decision by twelve people possibly gives fairer results.

- Juries have a reasonable track record for making the right decision.

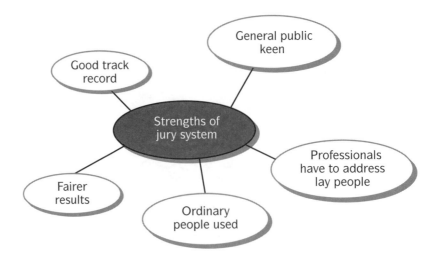

Strengths of the jury system

Index card revision

Summarize the points on strengths and weaknesses of the jury system.

Weaknesses of the jury system

● Juries may not represent a cross-section of the community.

● Jurors are not trained in their duties, apart from a brief video and some short leaflets.

● Some juries may find some complex cases difficult to understand.

● Jury service is compulsory, and some may find this disagreeable.

● Verdicts do not have explanations attached, so it is difficult to see whether the case was discussed properly and fairly.

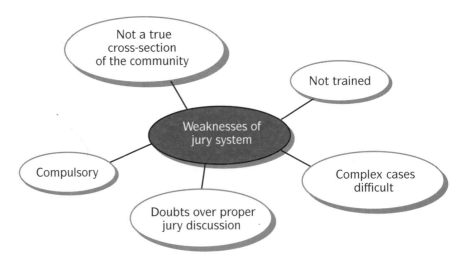

Weaknesses of the jury system

5 Alternatives to jury trial

This present system of jury trial is coming under pressure for change, Society has changed, the political system has changed, and even the types of offences committed have changed. Government is keen to see a cost-effective and fair system of trial, with the jury as a cornerstone of this.

Proposals already put forward have come in for fierce criticism from human rights groups and members of the legal profession. As a result of these pressures, the Government commissioned an important report which has taken two years to produce. The next section outlines some of its suggestions.

The Auld Report

The Auld Report affects not only magistrates, but also juries. Some proposals for reform include:

- smaller juries
- fewer disqualifications and excusals
- defendants losing some rights to be tried by jury
- greater support for jury members, with possible summaries of key facts
- allowing judges more power to overrule the decisions of a jury if he felt their decision was 'perverse'
- an attempt to make sure that juries reflect the local community by reducing the randomness of selection
- juries to be told of defendant's previous convictions.

The Auld Report was published in October 2001. The Government is now listening to the feedback it has generated and is soon to put some of its 300 recommendations into practice.

The Auld Report

The summary of the Auld Report contains the following key ideas for reform:

- 'A new national Criminal Justice Board should provide overall direction of the criminal justice system.'
- 'The Crown Court and Magistrates' Courts should be replaced by a unified Criminal Court consisting of three divisions.'
- 'Steps should be taken to provide benches of magistrates that more broadly reflect the communities they serve.'
- 'Jurors should be more widely representative than they are of the national and local communities from which they are drawn.'
- 'The defendant should no longer have an elective right to trial by jury. The responsibility should be that of the magistrate alone.'
- 'The current hierarchy of the judges and their jurisdictions should continue.'
- 'Four essentials are: strong prosecutors, efficient defence lawyers, access to clients by defence lawyers and a modern communications system.'
- 'Copies of summaries of the case should be provided to the jury.'
- 'There should be a single line of appeal from the Magistrates' Court and above to the Court of Appeal in all criminal matters.'

(Sir Robin Auld's Summary of his Review Report)

The Auld Report is calling for smaller juries

Group activity

Jill Dando was the popular presenter of the TV programme *Crimewatch*. She was shot dead on her doorstep after returning home from a shopping trip. After a huge police enquiry, the suspected killer was eventually arrested and taken to court. The jury found Barry George guilty of murder by a majority of 10-1 after many hours of discussion in the jury room. After the trial it was revealed that Mr George had a series of convictions for harassing women.

1 Do you think juries should be informed of the defendant's previous record, as the Auld Report suggests?

2 What effect would it have on the way a jury views a person with or without a record of previous convictions?

3 Will the jury give better or worse verdicts using this information?

Revision checklist

1 Jurors must be at least 18 years-old, be listed on the electoral role, and have lived in the UK for five years since the age of 13. People between 65 and 70 do not have to serve, and those over 70 not allowed to serve.

2 Some potential jurors disqualified: police, traffic wardens, barristers, solicitors, those connected to the legal process, people with mental illnesses and those who have been convicted of serious crimes.

3 Excusals do not have to serve if they choose not to: MPs, doctors, members of armed forces, those who have served within the last two years.

4 Discretion of judge: Parents with young children, people with pre-booked holidays, students with examinations looming.

5 Twelve jurors sit in a criminal case. Judge would prefer unanimous verdict (everyone agrees) but will accept a 11–1 or 10–2 majority after two hours and ten minutes.

6 Jurors listen to the facts of the case and decide the guilt or innocence of the defendant in criminal cases. In civil cases juries decide verdict and award damages.

7 Jurors may not really be representative sample of electorate due to excusals and disqualifications.

8 General public has faith in jury system but often not keen to participate.

9 Government keen to cut costs of jury trials, but human rights groups oppose changes.

10 Auld Report will affect role of lay people by weakening power of juries and strengthening power of magistrates.

Quick revision questions

1 Who can be a member of a jury?

2 Which groups of citizens are disqualified?

3 Who can be excused jury service?

4 Who can avoid their jury service at the discretion of the judge?

5 What are the duties of a jury in a criminal case?

6 What are the duties of a jury in a civil case?

7 List three weaknesses of the jury system.

8 List three strengths of the jury system.

9 Name the author of the recent review into the criminal courts.

10 Name three proposals from the review of the criminal courts.

Exam question

1 a How are juries selected? [20 marks]

b Is there a problem with the present jury system? [25 marks]

Exam answer guide

1 a Jurors must:

✓ Be on the electoral register

✓ Be at least 18 years-old

✓ Have lived in the UK for at least five years since the age of 13.

They are selected at random from the electoral register. Not all serve, however. Some people are disqualified, some people do not have to do their service if they choose not to, and some may be allowed to postpone if the judge allows.

b There may be problems caused by the disqualifications, excusals and discretions. This may not give a random selection. Juries may have too many older, retired people, people looking after others at home or those with time on their hands. The middle classes tend to escape service. There are plans to have no exclusions at all. Would this work? The Auld Review will change juries.

Government funding

Key points

1 Legal Services Commission (formerly Legal Aid Board)
2 Community Legal Service
3 Criminal Defence Service
4 Funding of civil and criminal cases
5 Advice schemes in civil and criminal cases
6 Access to justice

Why do I need to know about the financing of legal services?

Questions on this subject will ask about methods of financing legal advice and the problems individuals often have. You will need to know about the impact of the latest system of state funding resulting from the **Access to Justice Act 1999**. Questions will invite you to comment on the fairness and justice of the work of the Legal Services Commission and its two subsidiaries. Questions in this area will expect you to have views on how successful the changes have been. You will need to understand the structure of the new system, why it was introduced and its effectiveness.

Legal action can be expensive

1 Legal Services Commission (formerly Legal Aid Board)

The Legal Services Commission came into being on 1 April 2000. It replaced the old Legal Aid Board, which had done the job for over 50 years. The commission aims to meet the Government's objectives, which are: 'to promote and develop legal services that can be delivered within a controlled budget and to target them according to need'.

Group activity

We are all expected to obey the law. Should the Government therefore target publicly funded legal services or should everyone get support when they have a legal problem?

The Legal Services Commission makes contracts with providers of legal advice. The number of solicitors available under the scheme will only be around 5000, which is a significant reduction on numbers under the old system.

2 Community Legal Service

The Community Legal Service (CLS) now handles civil cases. It has a number of functions, including:

- coordinating the set budget through its regional offices, although there is a central fund for particularly expensive cases

- targeting funds at the most deserving cases

- providing general information about the legal system

- providing support in resolving disputes.

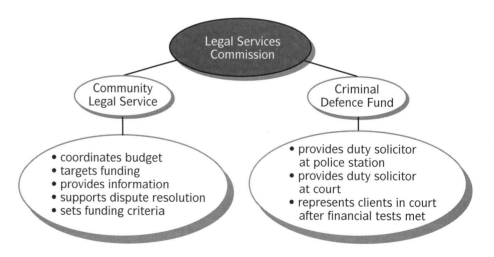

Legal Services Commission

Funding criteria

The funding of cases relies on a set of criteria laid down by the Government which the CLS has to use. They include the calculation of:

- cost versus benefit
- how much money there is left in the CLS fund
- importance to the public interest
- importance to the individual
- alternatives available to the individual
- the part the individual played in the case itself.

Contracts

From January 2001 organizations that wish to provide Government-funded legal services for civil cases must have a contract to do so from the CLS.

Conditional fee arrangements/'no win no fee'

This is one other important change which affects many people seeking legal advice. From 1 April 2000, the vast majority of civil cases are subject to 'no win no fee' arrangements. These are also known as *conditional fee arrangements*. Cases which fall outside 'no win no fee' are subject to a new funding code which gives priority to housing cases and those cases which involve a wider public interest.

Budgets are now strictly enforced

Web activity

Find the CLS web site on www.justask.org.uk. This site illustrates some of the support available to people with legal problems.

Exclusions from funding criteria

There are also a number of other exclusions from the system put in place by the funding criteria. There is no funding for cases that involve *conveyancing* (the buying and selling of houses), *last wills and testaments, trusts* (ways of avoiding tax on your wealth and income), *company law* and other business issues, *libel* (written lies about someone) and *slander* (spoken lies about someone).

Quick question

What are the criteria for funding a case?

3 Criminal Defence Service

The Criminal Defence Service is the second body under the control of the Legal Services Commission. Its aims are to: 'Secure advice, assistance and representation to those involved in criminal investigations or proceedings'.

Under this service, a duty solicitor is available free of charge to a person who is being detained or questioned by the police. This advice is sometimes only available via the telephone.

At the court a duty solicitor will advise defendants, again free of charge. They may also represent a person in court when there is an emergency situation. This may be when an application for bail is being made.

In general a Criminal Defence Service is available to all who need advice in the interests of justice and can meet the financial tests laid down.

Index card revision

Use index cards to summarize the work of the Legal Services Commission, Community Legal Service and Criminal Defence Service.

4 Funding of civil and criminal cases

The funding criteria for both civil and criminal legal aid ensure that the criminal cases take priority. These are the most serious court cases and often involve situations where a defendant could lose their liberty by being put in prison. If the funds of a regional Criminal Defence Service run out of money because of unexpected demand, resources are automatically diverted from civil into criminal.

Strengths and weaknesses of the present situation

The new system of Government funding of legal services is relatively new and probably needs some time to sort itself out. Some strengths and weaknesses are developing, however.

Strengths

- Funding is targeted to the more deserving cases via the funding criteria, with criminal cases taking priority.
- Information is more readily available to those who need legal advice via leaflets and Internet.

- Community Legal Service is planning partnerships with other national and local bodies to improve legal advice coordination.
- There is more consideration of mediation and negotiation services, rather than resorting to a formal court hearing.
- Conditional fee arrangements may encourage more people to seek a legal solution to an injury or accident.

Weaknesses

- Conditional fees may be more difficult to arrange if you have a weaker case, and it is argued that access to justice may be reduced.
- Fees may be high in relation to damages won.
- Some may find it difficult to meet the funding criteria needed in civil cases.
- It may be difficult to attract lawyers of the best calibre, given the pressure put on fees by Government spending limits.
- The quality of lawyers may deteriorate in the public system as payments for state-funded legal work lag behind private sector payments.
- Contracting of lawyers would reduce the pool of available legal advisers and could unfairly affect small, ethnic minority practices.

5 Advice schemes in civil and criminal cases

The Government was keen to make as much information available to the public as possible. Information technology was a relatively cheap and effective tool to use. A website 'justask' was established to offer advice on all services obtainable. The site has approximately 15 000 pages of information.

The Government is keen to organize the legal advice providers so that clients who need their help can access them quickly and easily. One of the tasks of the Legal Services Commission is to network these services. The main providers, such as Citizens Advice Bureaux and the Law Centres, can apply for contracts to provide Government-funded legal work. These are explained further in Unit 7.

There are many other ways of getting financial help or legal advice in addition to private purchase. Some are described in the sections below.

Household insurance policies

As part of the package protecting householders' possessions there is often a clause offering some element of legal insurance. A great many people are covered, but the numbers who know about or use this service may be much smaller.

Legal insurance

Specific legal insurance is quite common in other countries. It may become more common in the United Kingdom if the trend towards using the legal system more often continues.

Trade unions

Trade unions often retain a solicitors' firm to offer advice on employment issues, but a union may also have a facility to offer a set time period of advice to its members on other issues.

Citizens Advice Bureaux (CAB)

The Citizens Advice Bureaux provide a very popular free advice service which people are often happy to approach and use. There are close to 2000 outlets around the country. There are, however, two interrelated problems facing the CAB. First, their popularity puts a great strain on the resources available. Second, the resources available are inadequate for most of the outlets. They are victims of their own success and also demonstrate the huge demand for legal services that are convenient, informal and free of charge.

Web activity

Get onto the site of the Citizens Advice Bureaux at www.nacab.org.uk and look at the information on the range of services available at the CAB.

Law centres

There are only about 50 law centres and they face the same problems as the CAB, with huge demand and insufficient resources. Their popularity, along with the CAB, underlines the need for free and informal systems of advice. Law centres are normally set up in poorer areas to reduce the problem of unmet legal need amongst more disadvantaged social and economic groups.

Independent advice offices

There are close to a thousand small, independent legal advice centres covering areas such as welfare benefits, housing issues and debt advice. Often these are funded by churches, housing associations and charities.

Local authority units

Some local authorities provide free legal advice on a range of areas, including housing and social security benefits. They may also include a trading standards office, which can provide expert advice in consumer protection.

Pro bono

Pro bono means 'for free'. This practice is growing in popularity in the UK, helped by both the Law Society and the Bar Council. Free legal advice and representation are provided to needy individuals. *Pro bono* first gained prominence in the United States.

There were also a variety of political and media pressures to make the law simpler in terms of its vocabulary so that 'ordinary people' could understand

Law centres are always hard up

what was going on in the legal system. More use of Alternative Dispute Resolution (ADR) was encouraged, to reduce costs and make the legal process less formal.

6 Access to justice

Since 1949 the allocation and administration of state-funded legal advice and representation have been the responsibility of the Legal Aid Board. The Legal Aid Board had gradually become less efficient, and major financial and operational problems had begun to emerge. There were three key reasons for this.

1 Costs were becoming greater and greater. The number of people being helped, however, was in some years actually going down. The Government feared that unscrupulous lawyers were 'milking the system'.

2 Unmet legal need was not being cured. One of the main objectives of the Legal Aid Board was to ensure that those who needed support would get it. Even after fifty years, this was still a long way off.

3 Provision was unevenly provided between different Magistrates' Courts, and guidelines were not followed properly for the merit testing of cases. Access to justice was clearly being denied to some defendants.

The **Access to Justice Act 1999** introduced a coordinating body called the Legal Services Commission, which oversaw two new legal bodies: the Community Legal

Sources of legal funding

Service and the Criminal Defence Fund. This important piece of legislation fundamentally reformed access to Government-funded legal services for poorer members of society. It also brought some major changes to the legal profession – it allowed solicitors to speak in higher courts such as the Crown Court if they had the appropriate training and qualification. The qualification was called an Advocacy Certificate.

Web activity

For further information on the **Access to Justice Act 1999**, see the website at www.open.gov.uk/lcd and look for the section headed 'Access to Justice'.

Unmet legal need

Many people who might benefit from legal advice and representation do not, however, receive it. Some reasons for this situation have been identified. People may:

- not understand that they may benefit from a legal process
- not be able to find a convenient service to help them
- not be able to afford the service
- lack awareness of state-funded legal support or conditional fee arrangements
- lack the confidence to mount a legal action or even approach a solicitor
- overestimate the true cost of legal services
- have family or work commitments which prevent the pursuance of a case.

Group activity

Contact a local solicitor and see if they will give you information on the areas of law they practise in and how much typical cases cost. Possibly one letter or phone call per group would avoid overstretching the solicitor's secretary!

Revision checklist

1 Legal advice can be obtained in following ways: private purchase, insurance policies, trade union provision, Citizens Advice Bureaux and Law Centres, local authority provision and *pro bono*.

2 Unmet legal need exists because of lack of knowledge, lack of suitable service, cost, and pressures of work and family life.

3 **Access to Justice Act 1999** created three new bodies to administer Government funding and advice on legal matters: the Legal Services Commission, the Community Legal Service and the Criminal Defence Service.

4 The Legal Services Commission coordinates Government funding of legal services and attempts to coordinate legal providers.

5 The Community Legal Service deals with civil cases and manages a budget which is shared between various regions around the country.

6 The Criminal Defence Service deals with criminal cases. It provides duty solicitors at police stations and at Magistrates' Courts. It takes priority when there is a shortage of funding.

7 Funding criteria exist to allocate available funds to where Government thinks they should be targeted.

8 An important part of the new structure is the widespread use of conditional fee arrangements known as 'no win no fee' for personal injury claims.

9 *Conditional fee arrangements* allow the solicitor to charge the client for the cost of a normal case and then add a success fee to the total.

10 Some solicitors put a cap on the total charged so that clients do not see their damages swallowed by fees if those damages are low.

Quick revision questions

1 List six ways of financing or obtaining legal advice.

2 What is *unmet legal need*?

3 Name three reasons for the existence of unmet legal need.

4 What are the main duties of the Legal Services Commission?

5 What are the main aims of the Community Legal Service?

6 Why does the Community Legal Service have to use funding criteria?

7 What are *conditional fee arrangements*?

8 Name two benefits and two drawbacks of conditional fee arrangements.

9 What does the Criminal Defence Fund do?

10 Name two advantages and two disadvantages of the present provision of legal services by the Government.

Exam question

1 a What types of cases are funded by the Government? [20 marks]

b What are key problems with 'no win no fee' cases? [25 marks]

Exam answer guide

1 a The Government has decided to prioritize its funding of cases. Criminal cases, which may result in the defendant going to jail, are seen as more important. Civil cases are now mostly dealt with by conditional fee arrangements, so the work is put onto the shoulders of the client and the risk onto the solicitors.

b 'No win no fee' cases create problems for both client and solicitor.

For the client:

✓ It may be difficult to find a solicitor if a case is weak

✓ Solicitors may talk up the problems and increase their success fee

✓ Fewer providers under the new scheme.

For the solicitor:

✓ They get no payment if they lose the case.

✓ Work may be involved in examining cases they end up not taking.

✓ They may be forced to cap fees at too low a level.

The clear winners are the Government. They now have a system which has cut public spending and has possibly still improved access to legal services overall.

Advice agencies

Key points

1 Purpose and role of the Citizens Advice Bureaux
2 Law centres
3 Other advice agencies

Why do I need to know about advice agencies?

Knowledge on this topic will give depth to other areas of your work. This unit will link strongly with units on Government funding of legal services, solicitors and barristers, and the reform of the courts system. Advice agencies are very popular because for many the cost or the image of private services is a deterrent. You should understand the range of free advice available to members of the general public and be able to comment on the reasons for its existence. Some local research would be useful to identify what is on hand.

Free advice

1 Purpose and role of the Citizens Advice Bureaux

The Citizens Advice Bureaux (CAB) are the best known of the advice agencies serving the public. Each outlet is established as an independent charity funded by the local authority as well as charitable gifts from individuals, businesses and trusts. The CAB was established during the Second World War as an emergency service, but it has grown into a highly regarded and valuable national asset. There are 2000 CAB offices around the country, so it is likely that there will be one in your nearest town or city. There are 30 000 people working for CAB, 90 per cent of whom are volunteers. The service serves approximately five million people every year.

The National Association of Citizens Advice Bureaux

The National Association of Citizens Advice Bureaux (NACAB) coordinates the organization and owns each of the 2000 CAB outlets. It is funded by grants from the Government and by charitable donations. The NACAB organizes:

- the advice given in each of the 2000 outlets
- training for the 30 000 workers
- programmes that improve accessibility for all sections of the population to the excellent services of the CAB
- national publicity work with the media
- a national Advice Week each September which promotes its services
- campaigns in Parliament to improve legislation.

CAB – in great demand

The work of the CAB

Web activity

Find the NACAB web site on www.nacab.org.uk/aboutus and look up the page on social policy. It gives details of some of the aims and campaigns currently under way. The website also gives details on how you can become a volunteer worker.

Role of the local Citizens Advice Bureau

The Citizens Advice Bureau exists to provide free, independent and impartial advice to members of the general public. The areas it gives advice on are widespread and include debt counselling, consumer issues, social security and other benefits, tax matters, housing issues, legal matters, employment and immigration.

These are only a few of the issues the CAB will take on. In fact, it will take on any issue or refer the client to a suitable agency for further advice or representation.

Exam tip

You should try to quote and use official reports in your work.

In addition to giving advice, the CAB goes further. Its advisors will help clients fill out forms, write letters, negotiate with people who are owed money by a client and represent clients at court or in tribunals.

Clearly the CAB is at the cutting edge of issues affecting ordinary citizens, particularly those who cannot afford or do not have the confidence to access the services of professional legal help (see Unit 6 for further discussion of these issues). As a result it actively campaigns to change the law where it believes improvement is possible, particularly for those who are economically or socially disadvantaged.

Index card revision

List the main services offered by the local CAB offices.

The Citizens Advice Bureau has almost been a victim of its own success. It is so popular and well regarded by the general public that at times it struggles to meet the demand for its services. If Government wanted to challenge unmet legal need, an expansion of the funding given to the CAB would be a most effective policy.

2 Law centres

There are only about 50 law centres nationally, which often specialize in welfare issues and housing law. They enjoy the same informality and popularity as the CAB network. They also face the same problem of chronic underfunding. Typically the law centres are located in poor metropolitan areas and thus target a potential mountain of unmet legal need.

Web activity

Examine the work of the Law Centres Federation on website www.federationlawcentres.org.uk.

3 Other advice agencies

The CAB and the law centres are the two best known national organizations, but there are many other agencies and organizations offering advice on general and more specialized issues.

Trade unions

Trade unions often retain a solicitors' firm which offers advice on employment issues. In addition they may have a facility to offer advice to their members on general legal issues.

Independent advice centres

There are close to 1000 small, independent legal advice centres covering areas such as welfare benefits, housing issues and debt advice. Often churches, housing associations and charities fund these. Look up your *Yellow Pages* to see which advice centres operate in your local area and which groups they serve.

Local authority units

Some local authorities provide free legal advice on a range of areas, including housing and social security benefits. They may also include a trading standards office, which can provide expert advice in consumer protection.

Pro bono

Pro bono means that lawyers give their services free. This practice is growing in popularity in the UK, helped by both the Law Society and the Bar Council. Free legal advice and representation is given to needy individuals by lawyers who work for private law firms. *Pro bono* first gained prominence in the United States.

Pro bono

Media

Local and national media often take up stories of interest or offer advice through their columns. *Watchdog*, the BBC consumer affairs programme, is at one end of the spectrum and local newspapers covering local consumer and legal campaigns are at the other.

Revision checklist

1 The Citizens Advice Bureaux is the biggest advice agency, with 2000 outlets.

2 The CABs are organized nationally by the National Association of Citizens Advice Bureaux.

3 The CABs give advice on a range of issues that have a legal element, including: debt counselling, consumer issues, immigration, employment and housing problems.

4 CAB will sometimes represent clients at tribunals and even in court.

5 There are about 50 law centres giving more specialized legal advice.

6 Funding is often a problem for CABs and law centres.

7 Trade unions often provide legal services for their members.

8 Local authority units often specialize in consumer, housing and welfare advice.

9 Independent charities often target particular client groups when giving legal advice and some solicitors offer free legal advice (*pro bono*).

10 Media sources, such as national magazines, consumer affairs programmes and local newspapers often provide legal advice.

Quick revision questions

1 How are Citizens Advice Bureaux funded?

2 What percentage of their workforce are volunteers?

3 What are the main functions of NACAB?

4 What key areas does the CAB offer advice on?

5 What is the key problem the CAB network faces?

6 What do the law centres offer?

7 Where do law centres often locate their premises?

8 Apart from CAB and law centres, where else can advice come from?

9 What does *pro bono* mean?

10 How can the media give advice?

Exam question

1 a What are the key ways a person may obtain free legal advice? [20 marks]

   b Is there a solution to the pressure on advice agencies? [25 marks]

Exam answer guide

1 a Possible options could include:

   ✓ CAB

   ✓ Law centre

   ✓ Independent advice agency

   ✓ Trade union

   ✓ Local authority unit

   ✓ *Pro bono*

   ✓ Media

   ✓ Conditional fee arrangements/'no win no fee'.

You should understand the work of the CAB and law centres in depth. Use the other points to support your answer.

   b This part almost invites you to give an opinion, so do so:

   ✓ More Government or local authority funding

   ✓ Pressure/encouragement on legal service providers to do more

   ✓ Make welfare benefits and legal system less complex

   ✓ Encourage schools and colleges to provide training

   ✓ Greater participation of citizens to help each other

   ✓ Promote greater *pro bono* provision.

Lack of access and representation is a key civil rights question. Put forward a balanced but robust view on these issues.

UNIT 8

Role of the legal profession

Key points

1 Private funding of cases
2 Conditional fees

Why do I need to know about the legal profession?

The provision of legal services has been a topic of hot dispute for a very long time. Many find the system intimidating and most find it expensive. Questions in this area will ask about the effectiveness of Government reforms in bringing a competitive edge to the supply of legal services. The Government is slowly going down the road towards a one-lawyer profession in place of the present solicitor–barrister divide. The key question is whether the fusion of the two branches will benefit the client. Another ground-breaking area is conditional fees. Since the reforms brought in by the **Access to Justice Act 1999**, solicitors can take cases on a 'no win no fee' basis. This has totally changed the ballgame. Questions on this important new development can be linked into the area of unmet legal need and Government funding of legal cases.

Barristers and solicitors

1 Private funding of cases

The legal profession seeks to act as a guide and support to those who need to use the legal system. The system is complex and ever-changing, and even the most intelligent lay person will have difficulty keeping up with its procedures and developments. Two main providers of legal services are the solicitors and the barristers.

Up until very recently the professions of solicitor and barrister inhabited their own carefully separated worlds. Barristers acted as specialists in the higher courts, acting as advocates for clients. The solicitors acted as the general practitioner, dealing with a whole range of legal issues and seeking out expertise when needed.

The **Court and Legal Services Act 1990** and the **Access to Justice Act 1999** are seeking to bring about change in the world of the legal professionals.

Solicitors

Solicitors are the part of the legal profession best known to the general public. There are 80 000 solicitors operating in England and Wales, and most high streets have a number of solicitors' firms. Most solicitors work in private businesses, but about 15 per cent work for local authorities, the Crown Prosecution Service and other public bodies and large organizations.

Solicitors can work as individuals or they can form partnerships. Some firms can have over 100 solicitors, which allows individuals to specialize in areas that interest them. Solicitors are the general practitioners, and much of their private work falls into one of the following categories.

Advocacy

Advocacy means acting as advocate in court, particularly in the Magistrates' Court, representing clients.

Conveyancing

An important source of income for the typical solicitors' firm is dealing with the buying and selling of houses. This is known as *conveyancing*.

Last wills and testaments

This is not the happiest area, but an essential for those who want to be prepared and see their assets go to the ones they love.

Probate

Probate means sorting out the wishes of people who have died and making sure the right people get the goods.

Conveyancing: a key area of work for solicitors

Divorce proceedings

These can be difficult jobs, but many solicitors advertise 'non-aggressive' settlements.

Contracts

These agreements can cover a wide range of business and personal areas. They need to be accurate and legally binding and can be a difficult task at times.

Legal advice

Solicitors can offer advice in person, in writing or over the phone. The latter is now sometimes done by using premium-rate phone charges. The world we live in is becoming increasingly complex, and the provision of legal advice promises to be an area that will continue to grow.

Future for solicitors' work

Although the Law Society has lost some battles, the immediate future looks optimistic for solicitors. More rights to work in higher courts and proposed changes to the system from the Auld Review of the Courts look as if they may benefit solicitors.

Barristers

There are about 10 000 barristers working in England and Wales. They have three main roles.

Advocacy

The vast majority of barristers concentrate on working as advocates for clients in the higher courts. Their training is geared towards this activity and this is what most choose to do in their professional lives. Barristers have 'rights of audience' in all courts in England and Wales, which means they can deal with any cases in any court.

Preparation of opinion

The other main legal provision is the preparation of opinion. This means giving the barrister's view on whether a case is worth proceeding with and an assessment of the 'did you knows?' that may come out of it.

Commercial work

Some barristers are rarely found in court. They may specialize in an area of law such as tax, copyright law or company law. City firms may use the services of barristers and pay huge amounts of money for high-quality legal advice.

Future of barristers' work

The provision of services by barristers is clearly under tremendous pressure. Solicitors are being given more and more rights to move into areas of work that were once the monopoly of the barrister. The Auld Report 2001 may not be as kind to barristers as it is to solicitors. The reduction of rights to jury trial is not good news for those earning their living representing clients in the Crown Court. All these changes will eat into the livelihoods of the barristers. The Bar Council has a lot of work on its hands to defend the interests of barristers.

Pros and cons of having one professional legal body

The advantages of this scheme would include:

- cost to clients reduced
- client has to deal with only one legal expert
- specialization could still occur.

The disadvantages, on the other hand, would include:

- specialist advocacy skills blunted
- loss of the benefit of having a second opinion
- loss of a closely knit Bar community.

Changes affecting solicitors and barristers

2 Conditional fees

When solicitors work on a 'no win no fee' basis, it is known as a *conditional fee* arrangement. The client only gets charged if the solicitor wins the case. If the case is lost, the client pays nothing. The **Court and Legal Services Act 1990** first introduced conditional fees.

The **Access to Justice Act 1999** brought major changes for the Government funding of legal aid. The old Legal Aid Board was disbanded and the Legal Services Commission took over. One of the changes that came with these new developments was the use of 'no win no fee' for the majority of civil cases. Most people applying for funds from the Community Legal Service Fund were told to find a solicitor and arrange 'no win no fee'.

The 'no win no fee' system

The solicitor and the client estimate what the normal fee would be in the case before them. The solicitor is allowed to charge a 'success fee', which can be up to double the solicitor's normal charge. This must be negotiated between the client and the solicitor. This is known as *uplift*. If the case is lost, of course, then the client is charged nothing. To protect the client there may be a 'cap' put on the success fee. This is useful if the damages awarded are very low and avoids all the money awarded being taken up with solicitor's costs. The **Access to Justice Act 1999** allows all of the fees to be awarded, including the 'success fee', if the client wins the case.

If the client loses the case there is the problem of the other side's costs. It is possible to get an insurance policy to cover these costs. A problem arises, however, in that the cost of the insurance must be paid before the case is heard. Some people may not be able to afford this. It is possible now to recover these insurance costs from the losing party since an amendment to the **Access to Justice Act 1999**.

There are clearly strengths and weaknesses to this system of conditional fees/ 'no win no fee'.

Strengths include:

- Access to justice is improved.
- Winners can claim 'success fees' and insurance premiums back.
- Solicitors' costs may be capped.
- Only strong cases get through because solicitors will not take weak ones.

Weaknesses include:

- Solicitors may not take cases which are on the fence. They may prefer strong and winnable cases only.
- Insurance premiums have to be paid in advance, so even the strongest cases may not get to court.
- Cases can be complex and unexpectedly expensive. This puts solicitors at a disadvantage.

Revision checklist

1 Legal professionals are there to guide people through a complex system.

2 Barristers and solicitors have been kept separate but this is gradually changing. The Government is keen to see closer links.

3 The key work of the 80 000 solicitors is: acting as advocates in courts, conveyancing, drawing up last wills and testaments, dealing with probate, negotiating divorce settlements, drawing up papers and legal contracts, and offering legal advice.

4 The Auld Review promises to change the work of solicitors, for the better.

5 The key work of the 10 000 barristers is: acting as advocates in higher court, preparing opinion, and commercial work.

6 The Auld Review is probably not such good news for barristers. They may lose some of their work to solicitors.

7 A more fused legal profession would have the following advantages: reduced costs to clients, have to deal with one person, specialization could still occur. Disadvantages include: specialist skills reduced, second opinion lost, loss of a whole professional body.

8 Conditional fees are also known as 'no win no fee'. If the client loses, they pay nothing. If they win, the solicitor takes normal fee plus a 'success fee'.

9 'No win no fee' first started with the **Court and Legal Services Act 1990** but was extended with the **Access to Justice Act 1999**.

10 Advantages of conditional fee arrangement/'no win no fee' are: improved access to justice, winners can claim the success fee and other costs back, and only reasonable cases will be taken to court.
Disadvantages: solicitors may only take strong cases, insurance has to be paid in advance, and complex cases may leave solicitors out of pocket.

Quick revision questions

1 What Act of Parliament started the changes to the legal profession?

2 There are about 80 000 solicitors working in the English legal system. What is their main work?

3 There are about 10 000 barristers working in the English legal system. What is their main work?

4 What review is promising to bring further change to the legal profession?

5 What pros and cons are there to a single body of legal professionals?

6 What are conditional fee arrangements?

7 How are 'success fees' worked out?

8 Why are insurance payments that cover costs if the case is lost a problem for some clients?

9 What are the strengths of the conditional fee arrangement system?

10 What are the weaknesses of the conditional fee arrangement system?

Exam question

1 **a** Outline the conditional fee arrangement system. [20 marks]

    b Comment on the fairness of such a system. [25 marks]

Exam answer guide

1 **a** Key points about the conditional fee system:

- ✓ Was started by the **Court and Legal Services Act 1990** but greatly extended by the **Access to Justice Act 1999**
- ✓ Client has to approach solicitor to take case
- ✓ Fee is worked out with an element of reward called the 'success fee'
- ✓ Cap may be placed on solicitor's winnings, e.g. 15 per cent
- ✓ Insurance may be paid to protect against losing the case and having to pay other side's costs
- ✓ If solicitor wins the case, he or she gets his or her fee and client can claim damages
- ✓ If solicitor loses the case, client pays nothing.

b There are worries about the system:

- ✓ Weak cases may not be taken up by solicitors
- ✓ Fees may be inflated as solicitors stress 'weakness' of case to inflate success fee
- ✓ Insurance payments have to be paid before case.

On the other hand:

- ✓ Reduces risk for client
- ✓ Allows access to legal assistance
- ✓ Cap allows client to keep reasonable share of damages.

Analyse the issues and put your view.

Sources of Law

Doctrine of precedent

1 Judicial precedent

2 Lawmaking potential

Legislation

3 Acts of Parliament

4 Delegated legislation

5 Statutory interpretation

European law

6 European legislative process and institutions

7 Primary and secondary sources

Law reform

8 Impetus for law reform

9 Law reform agencies

Sources of law

UNIT 1

Judicial precedent

Key points

1 Precedent as operated in the English courts
2 *Stare decisis, obiter dicta* and *ratio decidendi*
3 Hierarchy of the courts
4 Binding and persuasive precedent
5 Overruling, reversing and distinguishing

Why do I need to know about judicial precedent?

An examination question about judicial precedent will be in the form of a case study. It will test your ability to apply what you know about judicial precedent to the material and ask you to comment on the whole process of using past cases. Judicial precedent goes to the heart of the power of the judiciary. You should therefore link this unit to Module 3 Unit 5 on Statutory interpretation, Module 2 Unit 1 on the Judiciary, Module 1 Unit 1 on the Civil courts and Unit 5 on the Criminal courts.

Judges are a source of law

1 Precedent as operated in the English courts

Most cases that come before a court are similar to cases heard before. There are probably only so many crimes and ways that they can be committed. If the facts of a case are similar enough, prosecutors, defenders and judges will use the legal arguments and decisions from these earlier cases. This is called using *precedent*.

Advantages of using precedent

There are some clear advantages arising from this approach.

Fairness

Each case is treated the same if the facts are close enough to each other. This means that there are no wild variations between similar cases. A person who commits a crime today will be treated the same as someone who commits a similar crime next year.

Consistency

There is consistency between cases that strengthens the system and also allows for some prediction of the result. Those contemplating crime will know that there will be certain consequences if they are caught.

Time-saving

Using precedent saves time for all those involved in the case. The arguments have already been analysed and decided upon.

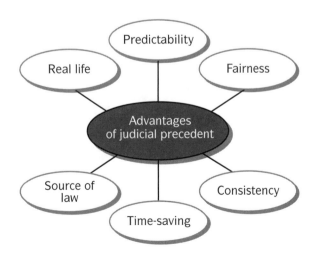

The advantages of legal precedent

Source of law

The system produces a valuable source of law within which legal personnel can operate. It provides a foundation for the legal system and is particularly useful for the training of lawyers. **Case law** provides approximately 400 000 examples of individuals and their stories within the legal system.

Real life

Case law is taken directly from real life. Law that comes from this source is not subject to problems of drafting and getting it wrong, which often happens with parliamentary legislation.

Disadvantages of using precedent

However, this approach has its disadvantages, too.

Vast choice of cases

Although the use of the Internet has improved the situation, the judge is still faced with a vast number of cases to choose from. Some cases are not, of course, yet on the system. These cases can only be used with the permission of the court they were heard in.

Inflexibility

Instead of looking at each case afresh, previous decisions have to be used. This might reduce the freshness with which each case is looked at. It also reduces the chance of law developing as society develops. What was criminal behaviour in Victorian times might not be seen in the same light in 2003.

Disputes

There may be disputes about whether the previous case applies to the new situation. Defence lawyers and prosecution lawyers may have very different views on which case is appropriate to use as an authority. The judge is left to choose.

The disadvantages of judicial precedent

Using precedent

The following cases illustrate how precedent has been used.

Legal case: *Donoghue v Stevenson (1932)*

Two friends visited a café, and one drank a bottle of ginger beer. When the last remains of the bottle of beer were poured into the glass, out came a decomposed snail. The woman felt ill and sued the manufacturer for this unpleasant experience. She won the case.

Exam tip

Questions will often ask you to comment on legal principles. This means looking at the pros and cons and giving your opinion.

Legal case: *Daniels v White (1938)*

The claimant bought a bottle of lemonade and when he drank it, he felt a burning reaction in his throat. The lemonade was examined and was found to contain a corrosive chemical. The case of *Donoghue v Stevenson* was used to win compensation successfully for the claimant, even though the case was slightly different. It was near enough, however, to use for the purposes of precedent.

Daniels v White (1938)

Glossary

Bind means that the judge has no choice but to obey. They are under an obligation to follow the lead set.

2 *Stare decisis, obiter dicta* and *ratio decidendi*

The legal system is full of rules and regulations which give the system its strength and its predictability. The process of making decisions on judicial precedent is helped by certain rules that are kept. There are three key conventions.

Stare decisis

Stare decisis means: Let the previous decision stand. Points of law that have been decided in previous similar cases must be followed. This makes the system consistent, fair and predictable. Another aspect to *stare decisis* is that higher courts take priority over lower courts, that is, decisions in higher courts are binding in lower courts. *Stare decisis*, therefore, allows previous decisions to influence later similar cases and ensures that higher courts **bind** lower courts.

Stare decisis also means that judges need information on previous relevant cases. The earliest records of cases date back to the thirteenth century. They were not particularly accurate! The Council of Law Reporting was created in 1865 to improve the process. It still produces Law Reports. Private companies also publish reports of cases. The most widely known is *All England Law Reports*. Electronic law reporting is now gaining popularity because of its incredible speed and accuracy. LEXIS is one system, but you will be able to find many websites on the Internet with past legal cases on them.

The *obiter dicta*

When making a judgment on a case, a judge may give many supporting arguments and explanations as to why they will come to a particular decision. This introductory stage, or anything else that is said by the judge which is not a central part of the judgment but is put in to make the situation clearer, is known as the *obiter dicta*. The *obiter dicta* includes:

- the judge's thought processes
- the judge's explanation as to why he or she arrived at one decision rather than another
- how the judge is going to apply the decision to the present case.

The *ratio decidendi*

Whereas the *obiter dicta* is the lead-up to the decision, the *ratio decidendi* is the core of the decision itself. This is the part of the decision made by the judge which has the effect of binding later courts. It is the piece later judges need to follow when looking at the case they are trying. The *ratio decidendi* is the core to the decision and is binding on the cases heard by later judges examining similar cases.

Quick question

What do the phrases *stare decisis, obiter dicta* and *ratio decidendi* mean? Write your answers on index cards and memorize them.

Group activity

Get a copy of *The Times* and find some law reports. Identify the *ratio decidendi* of some cases and note the court making the decision.

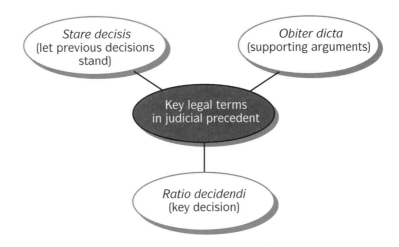

Key legal terms in judicial precedent

Exam tip

Be professional in
your legal studies.
Always take care to
spell legal terms
correctly.

3 Hierarchy of the courts

One of the fundamental rules of the concept of *stare decisis* is that higher courts
take priority over lower courts. The court system has a hierarchy. It has a
structure of power from the top to the bottom. Clearly, higher courts such as the
House of Lords can tell lower courts what to do. The higher court has more
senior and powerful judges sitting in it who can give orders and exert more
influence. The court system is organized as depicted in the flow digram below,
showing the most powerful court at the top. The Magistrates' Court also has
some minor civil jurisdiction.

In the civil system cases begin either in the County Court or the High Court,
depending on the amount of money involved, the complexity of the case and the
parties involved. The actual case is normally about who did what to whom, or

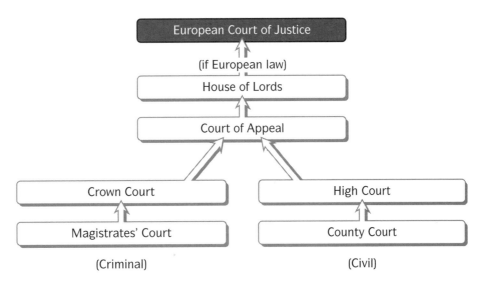

The hierarchy of the courts

how much A owes B. The case does not normally contest the validity of the law; it just looks at the facts of the argument.

If, when the decision comes, the losing party does not like the result or disputes the fairness of the law, the case can go to appeal. This begins what can be a lengthy and very expensive process. Normally only the rich or those backed by an organization such as a union or professional body go down this road.

Appeals are the place where precedent is more likely to be set. An appeal from the County Court or High Court can go to the Court of Appeal (Civil Division) or eventually to the Judicial Committee of the House of Lords. Whether a case becomes a precedent then depends on two things:

- The existence of a dispute over a point of law between two contesting legal parties.
- The ability and desire of both parties to pursue the matter further. If not, the legal point is not clarified and lives to be heard another day.

Inferior courts are those below High Court level. They cannot establish precedent. They follow the rulings of the courts above them. The Court of Appeal (Civil Division) and the Court of Appeal (Criminal Division) are not bound by each other. A ruling in *Young v Bristol Aeroplane Company (1944)* led to the civil division having flexibility to avoid some precedents.

The House of Lords is the highest court that sits in the UK and it sets precedent for all courts below it. It does not always have to follow its own previous decisions since the Practice Statement of 1966 which allowed it some flexibility in this area.

The European Court of Justice

The European Court of Justice (ECJ) is the highest court in the UK legal system where European law is involved. A case that starts in the County Court does not have to go through the full range of UK courts before it gets to Luxembourg, which is where the ECJ sits. It can go directly to the ECJ if the case involves a point of European Union law. When a decision is made by the ECJ, it is immediately binding on all UK courts.

Research activity

Using the law sections of national newspapers, identify the types of cases heard by the European Court of Justice.

4 Binding and persuasive precedent

Binding precedent

A judgment made on a case will contain various elements:

- the facts of the case
- a statement detailing the legal issues relating to the case *(ratio decidendi)*

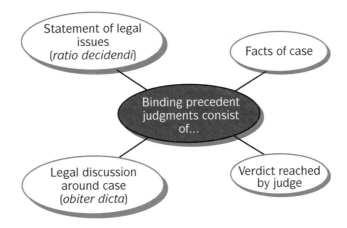

Elements of binding legal judgments

- the legal discussion surrounding the case *(obiter dicta)*
- the verdict reached by the judge.

The most important element is the *ratio decidendi*. It is this part which effectively binds the judges in later cases. The facts of the case can be used to see the relevance of the case, the *obiter dicta* can be used to understand the issues involved and the verdict may be of interest at the end of the hearing, but it is the *ratio decidendi* alone that binds the court.

Persuasive precedent

A *persuasive precedent* is a case that a court may use, but which it does not have to follow. The court may be *persuaded* to follow its legal rulings, but is not under any obligation to do so. Persuasive precedent may be:

- the surrounding legal discussion from an earlier case *(obiter dicta)*
- a decision that comes from a lower court in the hierarchy
- decisions from foreign courts, especially in Canada, New Zealand or Australia
- a judgment that was made in the Court of Appeal or the House of Lords which was outvoted by other judges on the panel. Dissenting views (those which go against the majority) in the English legal system are published, but not those in the European Court of Justice.

5 Overruling, reversing and distinguishing

The legal system reflects the society that it regulates. As a result, laws must develop and change if they are to be seen as fair and relevant. The law has developed to reflect more modern thinking on offences such as rape within marriage, the legal status of those with different sexual preferences and the official attitude towards taking drugs. The practice of judicial precedent has important flexibilities built into it to allow room for manoeuvre.

Overruling

Overruling involves higher courts creating a different legal ruling to one made by a previous lower court. The later case is looked at in a different way and the precedent set in the earlier case is set aside. The higher court destroys the earlier precedent when it does this and effectively declares the earlier ruling wrong. The House of Lords can also set aside its own earlier precedent. This was made possible by a device known as the Practice Statement 1966. This means that they are not bound by their own earlier decisions.

Overruling involves:

- two cases
- earlier decision on the first case discredited by the second case
- higher court makes decision to change precedent.

Reversing

If an appeal court overrules a decision made in a lower court on a particular case, it is known as reversing. A reversal is basically an appeal court decision which goes against the decision of the original court.

Reversing involves:

- one case
- case goes to appeal
- appeal court throws out earlier decision.

Overruling depends on hierarchy

Distinguishing

A judge who wants to avoid binding precedent set by an earlier case can try to argue that the facts in the two cases are different. If this is successful, the earlier precedent should not apply to the later case. The judge tries to distinguish between the two.

Distinguishing involves:

● two cases

● the judge does not want to follow precedent set in earlier one

● the judge claims the two cases are too different from each other to allow one case to set precedent in the other case.

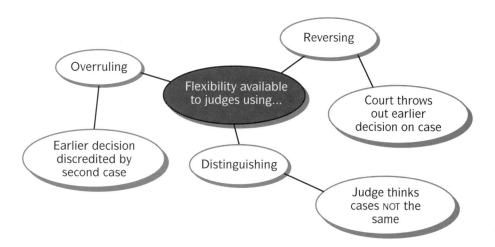

Judges can be flexible

Revision checklist

1 Precedent involves using the details and rulings of similar legal cases which have been heard before.

2 Advantages of using precedent are: fairness, consistency, saving time, produces a source of law, and involves real cases.

3 Disadvantages of using precedent are: too many cases to choose from, can lead to inflexibility, staleness and disputes arise over use of specific cases.

4 *Stare decisis* (let the previous decision stand), *obiter dicta* (words which support the core judgment) and *ratio decidendi* (the core judgment, the essence of the case).

5 The courts have a hierarchy which affects whether precedent is set. Higher courts bind lower courts.

6 Precedent is set when the case involves a dispute over the law and when the parties involved want to take the case higher.

7 The Practice Statement 1966 allows the House of Lords flexibility not to follow its own previous rulings.

8 Precedent set by the European Court of Justice binds all English courts.

9 Courts have to follow binding precedent but can choose to follow persuasive precedent.

10 Overruling involves a higher court setting aside a previous precedent; reversing involves an appeal court going against the findings of an earlier court on that case; distinguishing is when a judge tries to prove the case in front of them is substantially different from the case which is trying to bind them with a precedent.

Quick revision questions

1 Name the key advantages in using judicial precedent.

2 Why would a defence lawyer argue about which case should be used for precedent?

3 How can *obiter dicta* be used?

4 What are the advantages to using *stare decisis*?

5 What is the *ratio decidendi* of a case?

6 Draw the civil court structure.

7 What role does the European Court of Justice play in the English legal system?

8 What is the difference between binding and persuasive precedent?

9 What are the differences between overruling, reversing and distinguishing?

10 In what newspaper can you find law reports?

Exam question

1 a Outline the process of judicial precedent. [15 marks]
   b Why might precedent cause problems for the development of the law?
      [30 marks]

Exam answer guide

1 a The process of precedent relies on judges finding cases which have
      similar facts and then applying the earlier ruling to the later case. The
      judge may find information on previous cases from:
   ✓ The Internet
   ✓ CD-ROMs
   ✓ LEXIS
   ✓ *All England Law Reports*
   ✓ Law reports
   ✓ Newspapers.
   Lawyers will probably argue with the judge on which cases to use for
   precedent, but it is the judge who has the final say.

   b The following cases can be made.
   ✓ Precedent can be binding or persuasive. If it is binding it may limit the
     judge's ability to give new and fresh judgments. The House of Lords was
     once bound by its past decisions, which some people thought limited the
     scope for law development.
   ✓ On the other hand, judges can get around this by distinguishing the
     case, i.e. saying it is different from the one being tried. The higher courts
     can overrule and reverse decisions. The House of Lords can use the
     1966 Practice Statement to get out of its earlier decisions.
   Give both arguments and then state your own opinion. Is the use of
   precedent overall a beneficial state of affairs or not?

Lawmaking potential

Key points

1 Original precedent
2 The Practice Statement
3 Distinguishing
4 The role of the judges

Why do I need to know about the lawmaking potential of judges?

Questions about the creation of law by judges will expect you to know how they do it and the problems and benefits that arise from such an activity. Judges are an important part of the political/legal system. They need to be aware of the other two power centres: Parliament and the Government. Questions could ask you about the relationship between all three.

Judges create law

1 Original precedent

If a court hears a case involving a new point of law, it produces what is known as an *original precedent*. This means that future cases will follow that ruling. In a sense the judge has created a new law. In our legal system, many laws are created by the rulings of judges. This law is known as *common law*. It continues to develop by means of judicial precedent (see previous unit).

2 The Practice Statement 1966

The following of precedents set in courts has enormous advantages. There is, however, one key disadvantage. The courts may eventually feel themselves to be tied to out-of-date rulings which they would prefer not to follow. This is particularly a problem if the highest UK court, the House of Lords, is subject to the same pressure. All courts underneath the House of Lords have to follow its rulings. One of the fundamental parts of the idea *stare decisis* (let the previous decisions stand) is that lower courts follow higher courts. This would have eventually created a log jam of old-fashioned cases at the very top, with no chance of change.

To give the House of Lords some flexibility, the Lord Chancellor issued a new ruling in 1966 called the Practice Statement. It gave the House of Lords the chance to depart from its own earlier rulings. Up to this point the House of Lords was bound by its own earlier decisions (*London Tramways v London County Council (1898)*). The power would be used only after considering the effects on existing civil law, and the need for certainty in criminal law.

The House of Lords used the power given to it by the Practice Statement very infrequently at first. The first major case where the Practice Statement was implemented was *British Railways Board v Herrington (1972)*.

Legal cases: *British Railways Board v Herrington (1972)* and *Addie v Dumbreck (1929)*

The earlier case, *Addie v Dumbreck (1929)*, was about a child who was killed while trespassing near a mineshaft. The child was held to be at fault and the owners of the mine won the case. The later incident concerned a child who was badly injured after going through a gap in the fence onto an electric railway line. Attitudes had changed by 1972, and the House of Lords overruled the earlier case using the powers given to it in the Practice Statement 1966. The case now used for precedent would be *British Railways Board v Herrington (1972)*.

Another case that saw the use of the Practice Statement was *Pepper v Hart (1993)*, which concerned the use of **Hansard** to help with statutory interpretation. A third was *Hall v Simons (2000)*, which established the right to sue barristers for not doing their jobs properly. This overruled the precedent set by *Rondel v Worsley (1969)*.

Exam tip

It is always useful to write new notes. It organizes your thinking.

A case involving rape within marriage was brought before the House of Lords in 1991. Previous to the decision made in *R v R (1991)* it was held that rape within marriage was not a legal offence. Changing times made this view outdated, and the House of Lords overturned a legal position that had existed for centuries.

3 Distinguishing

The lower courts also have some flexibility. It comes in the form of *distinguishing*. This occurs if a judge decides that the present case is substantially different from a case suggested by the defence or prosecution. The judge does not need to follow precedent in these circumstances. This means the judge is free to choose another case or to create a new point of law using the process of original precedent.

The facts of the case should be significantly different if the judge is to reject a case suggested as a precedent. There is the possibility that a judge who does not like the details or outcome of the case suggested will be more inclined to see differences and therefore not want to use it. If there is a disagreement about which case to use, it may be further considered and settled on appeal.

4 The role of judges

The role of judges in creating law is fundamental to the English legal system. Parliament is the supreme lawmaker in the legal system, but judges have to interpret the law and they also create new points of law which are followed in later cases. The law created by judges is called *case law*. It is based on the decisions of cases already heard and decided upon by judges.

There are two jobs to be done when deciding a case.

- The material facts of the case must be identified and analysed.
- The law must be applied to those facts.

The application of law to a set of **material facts** is the task of the judge, and this is what creates case law. Once this has occurred, any case which has similar material facts will be treated in the same way by later courts. This produces fairness for the defendant since they are treated in the same way as previous defendants and it also provides some predictability for later potential offenders. They will know what to expect.

Glossary

The significant facts in a case are known as the **material facts**. When a judge distinguishes one case from another, the material facts must be significantly different.

Once the judge or judges have decided the line they are going to take, they prepare a written document which outlines their thinking and gives their decision. All views are put into the document, so if a judge does not agree with the findings, his or her reservations can be put down. This is known as a *dissenting view*. Even dissenting views are useful. Judges in later cases may consult all relevant views when interpreting a case.

English judges can dissent

Revision checklist

1 A court hearing a new point of law can create original precedent. All similar cases have to follow its ruling.

2 Law created by judges is called common law.

3 Common law is created by using judicial precedent.

4 The Practice Statement 1966 means that the House of Lords does not have to follow its own ruling. This frees the system up, since all courts have to follow the House of Lords.

5 The House of Lords is reluctant to use the Practice Statement because of the uncertainty caused in both civil and criminal law.

6 The first major case to use the practice statement was *British Railways Board v Herrington (1972)* and *Addie v Dumbreck (1929)*.

7 The lower courts have some flexibility by the use of *distinguishing*. This involves the judge showing that cases are substantially different.

8 Judges hearing cases have two main tasks: identifying material facts of the case and applying the law.

9 Judges put down their judgments in writing, including any views that are in a minority, or dissenting views.

10 The key part to the judgment is known as the *ratio decidendi* and any supporting information or arguments are known as *obiter dicta*.

Quick revision questions

1 Outline the meaning of original precedent.

2 What is the meaning of the term common law?

3 How is the 1966 Practice Statement used?

4 What case bound the House of Lords to its own past decisions?

5 Why were the House of Lords reluctant at first to use the Practice Statement?

6 What flexibility do the lower courts have, and how does it work?

7 What are the two main tasks for a judge when deciding a case?

8 What might be the benefit of including a dissenting view in a written judgment?

9 What is *ratio decidendi*?

10 How can *obiter dicta* be used in later cases?

Exam question

1 a How do judges create law? [20 marks]
  b Comment on the problems that may arise between Parliament and the judiciary when it comes to making laws. [25 marks]

Exam answer guide

1 a Judges follow earlier cases. This is known as *judicial precedent*. If they come across a new point of law, however, their decisions on the case effectively create new precedent. This is known as *original precedent*. Lower courts have to follow higher courts. The term *stare decisis*, which means 'let the decision stand', is used in these circumstances.

  b The French philosopher Montesquieu thought it best to separate powers in a country. He used England as an example as he felt Parliament, the Government and the judiciary were effectively separated. One of the problems with allowing judges to 'make law' is that Parliament and even the Government may feel their job is being taken over. The people elect the Parliament and the members of the Parliament (on the winning side) have some say on who makes up the Government. The judges are not elected. The fairness of their appointment is the cause for some debate, in fact. The question then is: Should we have laws made by elected representatives or by unelected judges? You must put your view forward in answering this question.

Acts of Parliament

Key points

1 Green Papers
2 White Papers
3 Legislative stages in Parliament

Why do I need to know about Acts of Parliament?

Although you have seen the growing importance of European law, English law is still the backbone of our present system. The vast majority of cases heard in court use English law. As a result you will be asked examination questions about the way that law is passed in the English legal system and also how English law is affected by our developing relationship with the European legal system. To understand fully the process of producing legislation, you need to know the main institutions in the legislation system and the part played by each. You should link this unit with those on the European Court of Justice (Module 1 Unit 3) and European legislative processes and institutions (Module 3 Unit 6).

Parliament, the supreme English lawmaker

1 Green Papers

When the Government wishes to hear from those interested in an area of law that it is planning to change, a Green Paper is issued. This is the first stage in the process of public **consultation**. Contributions from those interested are sent to the relevant Government department. The Government then has the opportunity to consider the points of view of both those who support and those who oppose the potential changes. Early consultation is seen as producing better legislation and allowing those who object to have their say. It may revise the ideas it first considered based on the feedback it receives.

2 White Papers

White Papers are issued after the Green Paper process is complete. The Government's proposals are firmer at this stage. Any relevant contributions it has received from its Green Paper process are incorporated into the White Paper. The White Paper offers more focused debate on the developed proposals. Eventually a *bill* based on the White Paper will be introduced to Parliament for its consideration. A bill is the name for a draft Act of Parliament. It will have to go through several stages before it becomes a law.

3 Legislative stages in Parliament

Draft Acts of Parliament come in two main forms, *public* and *private*. They can start in the House of Commons or the House of Lords (except for all important finance bills, which must start in the House of Commons). If the bill is to become law, it must go through a number of stages. Each stage improves the quality of the legislation and allows input from relevant contributors.

Public bills

The Government introduces most bills which come before the Houses of Parliament. These bills are known as *public bills* and attempt to meet the **manifesto** promises of the winning party. If the Government has a big majority of MPs, these bills will almost certainly be passed and become law. The bills are drafted by civil servants working in the department associated with the bill.

Private bills

Private bills focus on particular institutions or individual organizations. The institution or organization proposes them. A local authority might want to build a new road network or a modern tram system and may use a private bill. In the past railways were established by the use of bills. More recently a plan to change the ownership of the John Lewis shops failed because those involved did not have the resources to push a bill through Parliament.

Private Member's Bills

A small amount of parliamentary time is spent discussing *Private Member's Bills*. These are bills put forward by individual MPs. The bills reflect issues that are close to the hearts of the MPs putting them forward. Most successful Private Member's Bills have Government support. The majority of the bills put forward are non-controversial, but there have been some notable exceptions.

Quick questions

What is the difference between a public and a private bill?

1 The abolition of the death penalty came about from a Private Member's Bill which led to the **Murder (abolition of death penalty) Act 1965**.

2 The **Abortion Act 1967** was put forward as a Private Member's Bill by an MP called David Steele. The issues divided many people and are still the subject of controversy in some circles.

Stages in the progress of a bill

There are a number of steps in the progress of a bill.

1 A Green Paper is issued to act as a focus for discussion.

2 A White Paper is issued which builds on the consultation carried out from the Green Paper.

3 The bill is put before the House of Commons for three readings, a Committee Stage and a Report Stage.

   a The *First Reading* gives information about the name of the bill and its main intentions. A vote is taken in the house, usually verbally. If there are enough ayes (votes in support) the bill is carried forward to the next stage.

   b The *Second Reading* is the main debate on the bill's proposals in the House of Commons. Members of Parliament have an opportunity to discuss and debate, and to test the bill's strengths and weaknesses. There is a vote at the end of the second reading which determines whether it goes further or not.

   c The *Committee Stage* involves a more detailed examination of the bill. A committee of the House of Commons, reflecting the political strength of each of the main parties, sits and goes through this process.

   d The *Report Stage* allows MPs the chance to debate any changes introduced at the Committee Stage. If there are no changes, the bill will go through to the Third Reading.

   e The *Third Reading* is the final stage of the bill's progress in the House that it started in. If it started in the House of Commons, MPs will now vote on whether to accept it or not. It is very unlikely to fail at this point since it has already been through a number of stages where any opposition could have been examined and dealt with. This stage is normally a formality.

4 If the bill started in the House of Commons, it is now put before the House of Lords for the same process it went through in the Commons.

Exam tip

The highest marks are given to students who can accurately describe and comment on legal processes such as the passage of legislation.

Index card revision

Using cards, list the key stages in the progress of a piece of legislation.

5 The Queen gives her assent. This is another formality. The Queen does not even have the text of the bill in front of her since the **Royal Assent Act 1961**.

6 The Act of Parliament is now law.

Visit activity

The Houses of Parliament are open to visitors. You can watch the proceedings from the public gallery and may even get a guided tour if Parliament is not sitting.

Clearly this is a long and complicated process which has a great deal of scope for delay and confusion. Normally the whole process takes a number of months, although in times of national emergency legislation can be passed within a couple of days.

The House of Commons has the most power. If a bill goes to the House of Lords and there are problems with its passage, the House of Commons can overrule the Lords. The legislation used to do this is contained in the **Parliament Act 1911** and the **Parliament Act 1949**. The bill must be introduced to the House of Commons again and pass all the stages again. This clearly slows down the process and the Prime Minister and the Government do not look on it kindly. The House of Lords is now seen as a revising chamber and not there to oppose the Government of the people.

The Royal Assent

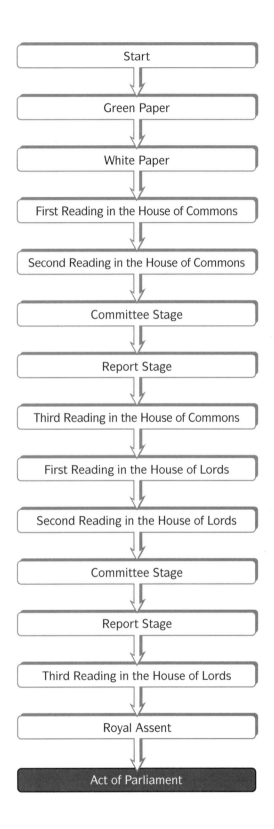

The passage of legislation

Revision checklist

1 Green Papers are used to start discussions on areas of law that Government is planning to change.

2 Contributors to Green Papers send their ideas or objections to the relevant Government department.

3 White Papers are produced after all comments on the Green Paper have been received and reviewed. They are firmer proposals.

4 Public bills come from Government and cover major promises made in the manifesto. Private bills relate to individual institutions or local authorities.

5 Private Member's Bills are started by individual Members of Parliament. They express the concerns of that member; unless they are supported by the Government they rarely make it to the end of the process.

6 The main stages in the progress of legislation are: Green Paper, White Paper, First Reading, Second Reading, Committee Stage, Report Stage, Third Reading, passed to the other House of Parliament for the same process, signed by the Queen and then finally law.

7 A bill normally takes a great deal of time to get through all stages, but emergency legislation can be passed within a couple of days.

8 The House of Commons is elected by the people while the House of Lords includes parliamentarians who have been given their jobs by politicians.

9 The **Parliament Acts of 1911** and **1949** allow the House of Commons to overrule the House of Lords if there is resistance to a bill.

10 If the **Parliament Act** is used, the legislation has to be reintroduced to the Commons in the next session of Parliament and pass all stages again.

Quick revision questions

1 What is the importance of a Green Paper?

2 What is a White Paper?

3 What are the differences between a public bill, a private bill and a Private Member's Bill?

4 Name a Private Member's Bill that has become law.

5 What happens during the First and Second Reading of a bill?

6 What does the Committee Stage involve?

7 What does the Report Stage allow MPs to do?

8 Outline details of the Third Reading.

9 What role does the Queen play in the passing of legislation?

10 What do the **Parliament Acts** allow the House of Commons to do?

Exam question

1 a Outline the key stages in the passing of an Act of Parliament.
      [20 marks]
   b How far does legislation reflect what the Government wishes?
      [25 marks]

Exam answer guide

1 a The key stages in the passing of an Act of Parliament are:
   ✓ Green Paper
   ✓ White Paper
   ✓ First Reading
   ✓ Second Reading
   ✓ Committee Stage
   ✓ Report Stage
   ✓ Third Reading
   ✓ Passed to other House of Parliament for repeat of previous process
   ✓ Queen gives assent
   ✓ Act is law.

   b The process of altering the bill probably starts with the Green Paper
      system, which allows outside feedback on the Government's proposals.
      Opposition parties (and the Government's own backbenchers) may try to
      change legislation at Green Paper/White Paper stage onwards.
      Committee Stage involving MPs from all main parties may add or take
      away from the bill. House of Lords may put amendments into legislation
      to change its flavour and even its direction. The Queen could refuse to
      sign the bill (but in reality would never do such a thing). All in all, there
      are many opportunities to influence and change the provisions and
      nature of the bill as it goes along.

UNIT 4

Delegated legislation

Key points

1 Orders in Council
2 Statutory Instruments
3 By-laws
4 Control of delegated legislation
5 Reasons for delegating legislative powers

Why do I need to know about delegated legislation?

Delegated legislation means allowing bodies beneath Parliament to pass their own legislation. Questions on delegated legislation focus on who is allowed to pass their own legislation and what controls are on them. You need to be able to analyse the system and the control devices that go with them, then give your opinion on whether they are a good or bad idea.

Delegated legislation

1 Orders in Council

Delegated legislation involves bodies below Parliament passing legislation for one reason or another. Orders in Council are laws passed in an emergency when Parliament is not sitting. The membership of this Council consists of the Queen and the **Privy Council**.

It used to be difficult to think of an occasion when Parliament would be so incapacitated that the Queen and the Lord Chancellor were making delegated legislation. The bombing of the World Trade Centre in September 2001 gave a chilling insight into the possibility of this happening. There were rumours that the Houses of Parliament were on the list of buildings to be attacked. If this nightmare had come true, Orders in Council may have been used as a last resort. The power of Orders in Council comes from the **Emergency Powers Act 1920**.

> **Glossary**
>
> The **Privy Council** is made up of senior politicians, including the Lord Chancellor. The **Judicial Committee of the Privy Council** is made up of senior judges and hears certain types of appeals.

2 Statutory Instruments

Government departments create Statutory Instruments (SIs). These are pieces of legislation which relate to the work of that department. These departments are given permission by using a **Parent Act**. The Parent Act gives guidance about how the new piece of legislation is to be written and processed.

A Statutory Instrument may be used by the Department of Transport to change road signs. The Health and Safety Executive may use one to change safety law. SIs give departments immense freedom to change the law and are used about three thousand times a year. They can become law in one of two ways.

> **Glossary**
>
> The **Parent Act** is also sometimes known as an **enabling act**. It enables the department to pass the legislation

Negative resolution procedure

After the SI is written, it is shown to Parliament. It is now technically a piece of law. If no one objects to its contents within 40 days, then it becomes permanent. If there are objections, then the SI must be debated in the House of Commons, the House of Lords or in a Standing Committee. It may be passed or it may be rejected.

Affirmative resolution procedure

If the SI is controversial, Parliament may put an instruction in the Parent Act that the issue has to be debated and voted on before it becomes law.

3 By-laws

Nottingham City Council, along with many other **local authorities** in the country, is enforcing a car ban in the City Centre area. Power to do this comes in the form of a piece of delegated legislation known as a *by-law*.

Other public bodies such as the railways can create and enforce by-laws. These are often about behaviour such as travelling without a ticket, behaving badly when drunk, or smoking on a train.

> **Glossary**
>
> A **local authority** is another name for a local council.

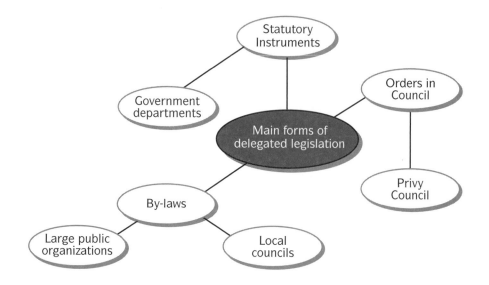

Types of delegated legislation

Research activity

Many by-laws are very publicly displayed, although most of the time people probably do not even see them. Over the next week see how many by-laws you can identify. Buses, trains and streets in town provide rich pickings.

By-laws

4 Control of delegated legislation

Giving power away does not mean that responsibility is given away. At the end of the day, Government picks up the blame if things go wrong. It is therefore keen to monitor and curb delegated legislation if it proves necessary. There are a number of ways that delegated legislation is controlled.

Scrutiny Committee

The Joint Select Committee on Statutory Instruments is responsible for checking Statutory Instruments and letting Parliament know of any problems. It is also known as the Scrutiny Committee (*scrutiny* means looking at something in close detail). Possible reasons for informing Parliament that there is a problem include:

- SI is going beyond its powers (this is known as *ultra vires*)
- SI is imposing a tax (which it is not allowed to do)
- SI is producing legislation which is unclear
- SI is producing retrospective legislation (backdating an offence).

Judicial review

All delegated legislation can be judicially reviewed. The case is taken to the Queen's Bench Division of the High Court and a High Court Judge is asked to decide whether the new legislation is in order or not. The most common reason for objecting to delegated legislation is that the organization acted beyond its powers (*ultra vires*).

Parent Act

The Parent Act which gave the power in the first place should be carefully drafted to make sure that defects and problems are reduced to the minimum.

5 Reasons for delegating legislative powers

Delegation means passing power downwards. In the English legal system this means passing power downwards from Parliament to organizations and bodies who need to pass laws.

- Government departments: for example, the Home Office may want to introduce new laws curbing criminal behaviour.
- Public organizations: for example, London Transport may want to launch new regulations such as a smoking ban on the Underground network.
- Local authorities: they may be introducing, for example, car-free city centres.

There are a number of reasons why Parliament is happy to allow these various organizations to consult on, draft and introduce their own legislation.

Limited parliamentary time

Parliament has a limited amount of time to pass legislation. The Government chooses to push its own major legislation through Parliament. Each Government makes certain promises in its manifesto. If it is to retain its credibility, it must keep at least some of the promises it made before the election.

Local knowledge

Parliament may feel that it is not the best institution to recognize and deal with the needs of local people. Politicians called *councillors* are elected by local people to run local authorities. It is in the interests of councillors to pass legislation known as by-laws to satisfy local needs if they are keen on re-election!

Specialization

Parliament contains MPs from a wealth of backgrounds. They cannot, however, be expert on everything. There are times when only the professionals can do it if you want the job completed properly. The **Social Security Act 1984** brought about complex changes in the payments of Income Support. Professionals in the Department of Social Security developed the legislation and also reviewed its effectiveness.

Limited parliamentary time

Fast response

Delegated legislation can often respond to changing needs more quickly than a full passage through the parliamentary system. Most bills take at least several months to go through the many stages needed, even when there is no opposition to them.

Delegated legislation can be completed much more quickly. A new system for paying Income Support benefits came into force in 1987. There were to be no payments of Income Support to anyone under the age of 18.

This new system caused great hardship to some unsupported younger people. Within a few days, a new system of hardship payments came into force. This was an example of a very rapid response, using delegated legislation to amend the law.

Future needs

Drafters of legislation cannot foresee the changes that may come about in the future. Delegated legislation can be used to amend legislation more quickly and more effectively.

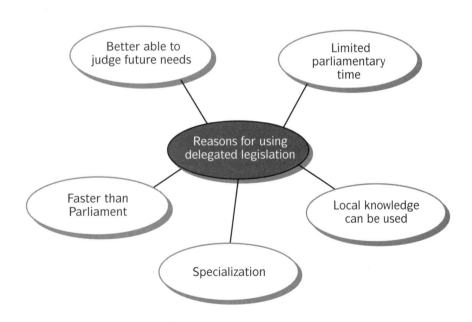

Why delegate legislation?

Revision checklist

1 Delegated legislation saves time in Parliament that can be used for 'more important' pieces of legislation.

2 Parent Act/enabling act gives guidance on what can be put into a particular piece of delegated legislation.

3 MPs in all fields are not experts, so delegation allows the use of expert civil servants or other professionals to explore the details.

4 Delegated legislation allows a quick response to changing circumstances or mistakes.

5 Delegated legislation is scrutinized by committees who have time to look into details of the legislation.

6 Delegated legislation is drafted by unelected civil servants in powerful government departments.

7 Councillors are local politicians who push delegated legislation through at a local level.

8 The Privy Council produces Orders in Council. The Council consists of the monarch, senior politicians and senior judges.

9 Main forms of delegated legislation are Orders in Council, Statutory Instruments and by-laws.

10 Delegated legislation is covered by Judicial Review.

Quick revision questions

1 Who are the main players in Orders in Council?

2 Who produces Statutory Instruments?

3 What are by-laws?

4 Who uses by-laws?

5 What does the Scrutiny Committee do?

6 What are the main reasons for finding a problem with a piece of delegated legislation?

7 When are Judicial Reviews normally used with delegated legislation?

8 Who are the main users of delegated legislation?

9 Why is delegated legislation such a good idea?

10 What is a Parent Act?

Exam question

1 **a** Who are the main users of delegated legislation? [20 marks]

b Should all legislation go through elected bodies? [25 marks]

Exam answer guide

1 **a** Main users include:
- ✓ Government departments
- ✓ Local authorities
- ✓ Public bodies.

Give examples of the types of use delegated legislation is put to.

b Although Government departments are not directly elected, the head of the department, the Minister, is. Local authorities contain elected members called Councillors. They obviously keep an eye on what the Chief Executive of the Council is up to in their name. Public bodies are not elected but their work is monitored by the Scrutiny Committee and presumably by the regulatory body attached to their industry. The general public is also fairly effective in bringing bad law to the attention of their elected representatives, or at least to the attention of the local newspaper.

UNIT 5

Statutory interpretation

Why do I need to know about statutory interpretation?

Statutory interpretation questions will focus on what powers the judges have to make sense of the law when there are ambiguities or absurdities. The power of

Statutory interpretation

statutory interpretation is a powerful one since in some ways it means that judges can stand in for the supreme lawmaking institution of Parliament. Judges have different approaches. You will need to know these and apply them in the case study material you will be presented with in the examination.

1 Statutory interpretation

The process of working out the meanings of the words in Acts of Parliament (**Statutes**) or in other legislation is known as *statutory interpretation*. Parliament passes laws and allows judges to put them into operation.

Drafting legal documents is a time-consuming and difficult task. Sometimes the more you look at a piece of writing that you have done, the less you see. With legal documents, accuracy and clear meaning is of great importance. With most things in life, however, tiny mistakes creep in or things happen that you could never have imagined. It is left to judges to interpret the law. In other words, judges must use their experience and skill to make the best use of sometimes imperfect law to ensure a fair and just outcome to a case.

Some help is given to judges from within the legislation itself. Some help also comes from following certain rules. Additionally, the passing of the **Interpretation Act 1978** has provided judges with guidance to help them in this difficult task.

Problems of interpretation

There are a variety of reasons why judges need to interpret the law to bring out its full meaning.

Subtleties of language

The subtleties of language encourage disputes about the meanings of words. English is particularly disposed to this, and legal language adds another dimension. Even ordinary words spelt exactly the same often have different meanings. The word *jumper* can refer to someone hopping up and down or to an item of clothing. The word *shoe* could mean something you wear on your foot or putting a piece of metal on the bottom of a horse's hoof. There are thousands of examples of words that have a double meaning, and no matter how hard the writers of law try, they cannot avoid including some. The position is not helped when lawyers deliberately attempt to seek out and manipulate these confusions to support their client.

Passage of time

The passage of time can make some words redundant or change words from their original meaning. Some laws remain on the books for decades or longer, so the scope for this is great. This is probably another reason for legal terminology sounding so old-fashioned and out of date.

Unclear meaning

In normal communication you can ask the other person to clarify what they mean, but this is impossible with the law. The lawmakers cannot be contacted after the law has been passed and questioned about what they meant. Judges have to do their best to uncover the meaning or investigate if it is unclear.

New situations

New inventions and new situations mean that legislation is sometimes used in unfamiliar circumstances. Judges then need to use the law flexibly. This is often the case with technological or social changes. The use of e-mail, the Internet and certain recreational drugs has forced judges to use existing laws until new ones can be produced.

Different perspectives

Our own racial, religious, social, political and family perspectives make us see words, ideas and laws in different ways. The judges must do their best to find some common ground on the meaning of the law.

2 Literal rule

There are three broad approaches to the interpretation of legislation. A judge may choose which one to adopt, or may even use all three at different stages in the interpretation. The first is the literal rule.

The literal rule involves looking at the dictionary definition of the words and using these ordinary meanings, even if the result is illogical or silly. This approach has some advantages, however.

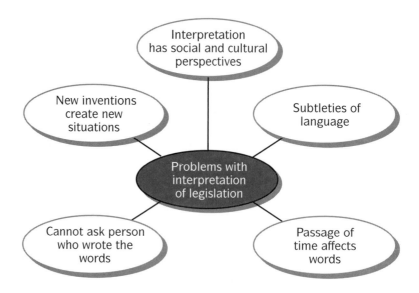

Why judges have to interpret the law

Advantages of the literal rule

Certainty

We can all probably agree on the ordinary meaning of words and the 'meaning' of the law is not interpreted or interfered with by the judges. They obey the strict letter of the law.

Reduction of litigation

Laws are often tested in the court to clarify or even change their meanings. The literal approach makes this testing a waste of time.

Constitutional position

If judges obey the letter of the law, no one can say they are defying the right of Parliament to have its will done. Parliament is the supreme lawmaker, and the literal approach helps it maintain this position.

Disadvantages of the literal rule

There are some disadvantages of using the literal rule, however.

Uncertainty of words

The rule does not take into account the nature of language. The words we use have ambiguities attached to them which we experience every day.

Problems of drafting law

People are not perfect, including those who draft our laws and even those who make them. Mistakes will be made no matter how hard they try. The job of the person drafting legislation is to minimize the errors as much as possible, but there will always be some mistakes.

Lack of flexibility

Flexibility is the key to all effective and long-lasting systems. The literal approach avoids this suppleness and may make the legal system unfair and open to damage.

3 Golden rule

Another approach to interpretation is the golden rule. If the legislation throws up two possible meanings or an absurdity, the golden rule says to choose the one which is least bizarre or look for the sensible meaning. The golden rule was defined by Lord Blackburn in 1877 when he said that the court should take the literal meaning unless it led to an absurdity. If this was the case, then the court should use its common sense and choose the most sensible meaning.

There is a problem, however, with the golden rule if a judge thinks it is an absurdity because they do not like the law. They may then see absurdities where perhaps none exist.

Legal case *R v Allen (1872)*

Allen was a man accused of bigamy, which means marrying a person while you are still married to another. The law seemed to suggest that he could not marry a second time as he was already married. This would mean that no one could ever commit the offence of bigamy. The law was interpreted to mean 'going through with a marriage ceremony'. Allen was found guilty.

4 Mischief rule

The mischief rule is the other approach to interpretation. It attempts to understand what Parliament meant: what wrong or mischief the law was trying to correct. For example, the **Theft Act 1968** attempts to prevent people from stealing and ensure that ordinary citizens do not lose their property. If a misleading paragraph in the legislation went against this and rewarded the thief and punished the innocent victim, then the court would know there was something wrong if it used the mischief rule.

A key case in developing the mischief rule was *Heydon's Case 1584*. The case encouraged judges to:

- look at the previous law
- explore what was wrong with that law

R v Allen (1872)

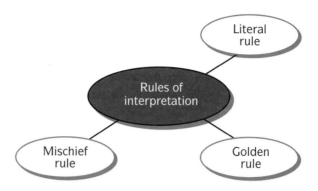

The rules of interpretation

- identify how Parliament intended to bring about improvements
- apply the findings to the case they were considering.

Smith v Hughes (1960) shows how the mischief rule was used more recently.

Legal case: *Smith v Hughes (1960)*

In 1958 the law made illegal the practice of prostitutes using the street to find customers for their services (soliciting). The law specifically mentioned 'streets'. A defence was put up that the prostitute was *hanging out of her window* overlooking the street and was therefore innocent of breaking the law. The court used the mischief rule and declared that it was the will of Parliament to avoid the nuisance caused by the actions of the prostitutes, whether in the street or hanging out of windows.

5 Purposive approach

The latest development of these three ways of interpreting is called the *purposive approach* (looking for the purpose). It is very much along the lines of the mischief approach in looking for what Parliament intended. and applying it to the case in hand. The starting point for the process of interpretation is, of course, still the words themselves.

Legal case: *Royal College of Nursing v Department of Health and Social Security (1981)*

The **Abortion Act 1967** made abortion legal for the first time in the UK. There were a number of conditions attached when the law was passed. One of these was that a 'registered medical practitioner' performed the operation. This was taken to mean a doctor. Over the years drugs were developed which meant that nurses were more than capable of performing and monitoring the procedure. The law lords came to the conclusion that the intention of Parliament was to avoid illegal abortions ('back street' abortions). This meant that nurses could now perform the procedure since they worked in a legitimate medical environment.

Exam tip

Although these approaches are called 'rules', judges actually have choice about whether to use them or not.

Index card revision

Using index cards, note the three rules of interpretation used by judges. Even if you have difficulty remembering the phrases, try to remember the concepts.

Group activity

The 'morning after' pill can be bought over the counter at chemists' shops or obtained free on prescription from doctors' surgeries. Do you think this development means the issue of abortion methods and presence of a medical practitioner needs clarification in court?

6 Rules of language

Clearly the interpretation of law has always been an issue. Some rules and guidance have come about to help.

The *ejusdem generis* principle means that a word takes its meaning from the words around it. A list of words referring to cars, such as hatchback, sports, saloon, convertible, family, will not then include a two-wheeled motorbike. The general word takes its meaning from the specific words mentioned as examples.

The *expressio unius exclusio alterius* principle means the inclusion of one type of item excludes others. The **Channel Tunnel Act 1986** refers only to that one tunnel and not to others that may be constructed.

The *noscitur a sociis* principle means that the word should be interpreted within the context. The paragraph, section or Act itself will give guidance as to the word's meaning.

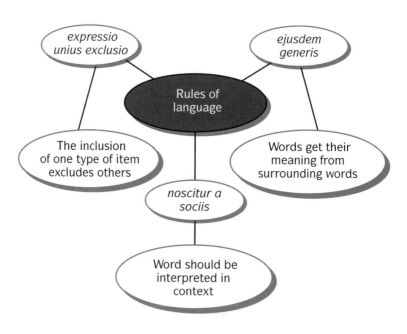

The rules of language

7 Presumptions

There are three key assumptions that the judge will take for granted when interpreting the law. These presumptions will hold unless it can be argued that they should not.

1 *Mens rea* (the mental element) is required for a crime to be committed.

2 The common law has not changed.

3 There is no retrospective law (you cannot be charged with an offence that did not exist when you carried it out).

8 Intrinsic and extrinsic aids

Intrinsic aids

These are aids which are internal to the legislation. They are present inside the Act of Parliament itself to help with the interpretation of the law.

- *The name of the Act* gives the objectives of the piece of legislation and at times can be long and detailed to avoid misinterpretation of these objectives.

- Sometimes there are *detailed definitions* of the words used in the Act to ensure everyone is focused on the right meaning.

- Marginal notes are used to guide the reader in the right direction.

- There are interpretation sections which give guidance on areas where there may be problems.

Extrinsic aids

These are aids which are external to the legislation.

- The *Oxford English Dictionary* is particularly useful if judges are making use of the literal rule. It can, of course, help in all situations to have a definition of legal terms from such a reputable source as the OED.

- Official government documentation such as Green Papers (first draft ideas) and White Papers (later firmer proposals for discussion) can be useful.

- Law Commission Reports give information on the reasons for possible changes in the law, and judges may use these sources to better inform themselves of the origin of the concern that led to a change in the law.

- Other statutes (Acts) which relate to or went before the one they are exploring give judges a context to use when considering the case being interpreted.

- *Hansard* is the official record of parliamentary debates. All speeches and statements are written down in its record. It may be useful for judges to read the debates by members of the House of Commons or House of Lords that went before the passing of the Act. It may give some context and insight into the reasons for the law.

Extrinsic aid

Web activity

Look for *Hansard* on the web. Explore the details of a debate to see the format that is used in parliamentary debates.

Legal case: *Pepper v Hart (1993)*

Confusion over the meaning of the **Finance Act 1976** meant that teachers who were possibly entitled to a tax allowance seemed to be losing out. The court eventually went to the record of the debate in Parliament which made it clear what the intention of the legislation was. This was a breakthrough in the use of *Hansard* for court use. The teachers got their tax allowance.

The publications of pressure groups cannot be used to inform the decision. Only official publications are allowed.

9 Effects of EU membership on interpretation

There have been changes over time in what is seen as the most fashionable method of interpreting legislation. The present trend is towards a more purposive approach. This has partly come about because of a more flexible attitude towards interpretation, giving the mischief rule more priority over the literal rule, but also because of the influence of the European Union.

The European Court of Justice has a purposive attitude towards the interpretation of law. The interpretation of European law is supported by frequent reference to official European Parliamentary and institutional sources. This has had its effect on the operations of the English judiciary. They are under an obligation to interpret European law with the purposive approach, and now tend to use this approach with English law also. In addition, English courts can make use of a variety of extrinsic (external) aids, including international conventions and *travaux préparatories* (preparatory legal materials). All of these developments have moved the interpretation of law away from literal interpretations and towards the purposive camp.

Revision checklist

1 The interpretation of law is required because: there are ambiguities in language, we are not able to clarify law with the makers, new situations arise, words are bound up with cultural values.

2 Judges attempt to interpret the meaning of the law and are helped by the **Interpretation Act 1978**.

3 Three approaches (or rules) to interpretation include: literal, golden and mischief.

4 Approach most in favour now called purposive, which is very similar to the mischief rule.

5 Rules of language: *ejusdem generis* (word takes meaning from those around), *expressio unius exclusio alterius* (inclusion of one type excludes others), and *noscitur a sociis* (word must be interpreted within context).

6 Presumptions when interpreting law: *mens rea* required, common law has not changed, and no retrospective law.

7 Intrinsic (internal) aids include: name of the act, definitions of words, notes in the margins, and interpretation sections.

8 Extrinsic (external) aids include: dictionaries, official relevant government publications, Law Commission Reports, other statutes and *Hansard*.

9 European Union membership has encouraged purposive approach to interpretation. European Court of Justice takes this approach.

10 English courts use a variety of extrinsic aids, including international conventions and preparatory materials.

Quick revision questions

1 What are the main causes of disputes about the meaning of legislation?

2 Name some advantages to the literal rule.

3 What is the golden rule?

4 What did *Heydon's Case* illustrate?

5 What is the purposive approach?

6 What do the following terms mean:

- *ejusdem generis*

- *expressio unius exclusio alterius*

- *noscitur a sociis*?

7 What are the three main presumptions judges make when interpreting?

8 Name some intrinsic aids.

9 Name some extrinsic aids.

10 What approach does the European Court of Justice take to interpretation of legislation?

1   a   Outline the meaning of the term *literal rule*. [20 marks]
    b   Comment on the problems that might arise in using the literal rule.
        [25 marks]

Exam answer guide

1   a   The literal rule relies on using the dictionary definition of words contained
        in legislation. It looks only at the meaning of the words used and not
        their context or the intention of the legislators. There are some
        advantages of the literal approach, including:
        ✓ Certainty of meaning, with the use of commonly used words
        ✓ Reduction of litigation, since there are no legal terms to clarify in court
        ✓ Constitutional position: it means the courts are not going against the will
          of Parliament.
This is an approach which is losing favour, partly due to a more flexible
approach from judges in the interpretation of the law but also because the
European Court of Justice favours the purposive method.

    b   Significant problems may arise in using the literal approach:
        ✓ Uncertainty of word meanings means that the literal approach may bring
          about an unjust interpretation of the law.
        ✓ Problems of drafting law mean mistakes will always be present. Possibly
          judges should attempt to iron these out.
        ✓ Lack of flexibility means judges do not use common sense, even when
          the meaning may be clear to all.
Part b contains the bulk of marks for this question, so concentrate your
resources here and comment on the literal approach.

European legislative processes and institutions

Key points

1 The functions of the Council
2 The Commission
3 Parliament
4 The role and composition of the European Court of Justice

Why do I need to know about European institutions?

The English legal system was profoundly changed in 1972 when the UK joined the European Community. Questions on this area of law will ask you about the roles of the various European bodies and typically about issues of who has the most power and jurisdiction. The **European Communities Act 1972** (effective from 1 January 1973) fundamentally changed the relationship between European institutions and English institutions. You will be expected to have a balanced and informed view on the various European institutions.

Two systems of law

1 The functions of the Council

The European Union

The European Union is a group of powerful Western European countries who have been drawn closer to each other by a set of agreements. These agreements cover important areas such as economic, business, trade and even military issues. The countries believe that they are more powerful and more prosperous when they act as a group rather than as individual countries. The cement that holds these agreements together is European Union law.

The Council of Ministers

The main decision-making and lawmaking body of the European Union is the Council of Ministers. As a result, this is the most powerful part of the European Union structure.

The number of votes each country has is based on its total population. To ensure fairness, the five big countries always have to get the support of smaller countries to win a vote. This ensures that smaller members have their say and that the big countries do not always win issues beneficial to them. This is known as *weighting*.

Member states normally send their Foreign Ministers as their representatives to the Council of Ministers. Each Foreign Minister will speak for the interests of his or her country within the Council of Ministers.

The Council of Ministers

Since Foreign Ministers have many other responsibilities back at home, there is a committee of diplomats who act as representatives when the Foreign Ministers are not there. They do the day-to-day work so that when Ministers do meet they discuss only the most important and urgent matters. The committee is known as The Committee of Permanent Representatives.

Some meetings of the Council of Ministers discuss specific issues. These meetings may be better dealt with by a minister from a particular department. If, for example, the Council is discussing the beef ban caused by BSE or the spread of foot-and-mouth disease in Europe, then the Agriculture Minister from each member state would attend the meeting instead.

Finally, if the Prime Ministers of the member countries meet, the meeting is called a *summit*.

2 The Commission

The European Commission acts on behalf of the interests of the European Union. Although each Commissioner comes from a member country, he or she puts aside the interest of their own country and focuses on the interests of all fifteen European member states.

The Commission consists of twenty Commissioners. The big five countries, Germany, France, United Kingdom, Spain and Italy, have two Commissioners each, whilst smaller countries, such as Luxembourg, have one Commissioner each. Each Commissioner holds his or her post for five years and has responsibility for a particular area. One of our Commissioners, Neil Kinnock, is Vice-President of the Commission.

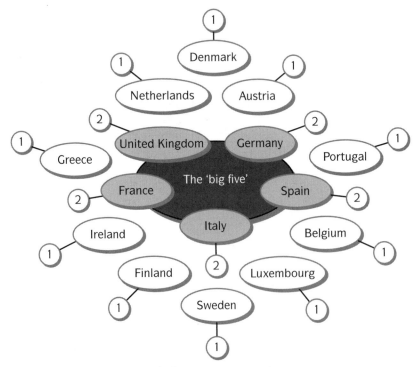

Countries and European Commissioners

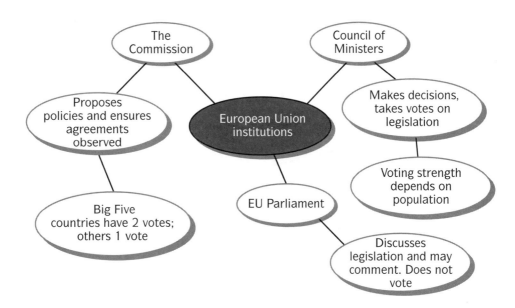

The institutions of the European Union

The key jobs of the Commission are:

- Proposing policies for The Council of Ministers to discuss. The policies take a European view that may not always fit with what each member of the Council might believe. It is always possible that a conflict could arise between what one country believes should happen and what the Commission would like to see.

- Ensuring that agreements reached by member states of the European Union are carried out. It is no good passing a law if no one follows it. If there are serious problems, the Commission can refer the matter to the European Court of Justice (see section 4 of this unit).

- Dealing with the immense budget of the European Union.

- Investigating the behaviour of large businesses operating in the European Union. The EU hopes to ensure fair competition and practices and is one of the few organizations in the world with the power to take on large multi-national companies, who may be exploiting consumers or other companies.

3 Parliament

The European Parliament is very different from our own House of Commons and House of Lords. The European Parliament is a place for discussing and commenting on the legislation that is passing through the European legislative system. This process is known as **consultation**.

The European Parliament does, however, have some important powers. For example, it has the power to investigate the Council of Ministers and the Commission. It can also dismiss the Commission and has the right to refuse the choices of Commissioner put forward by particular countries.

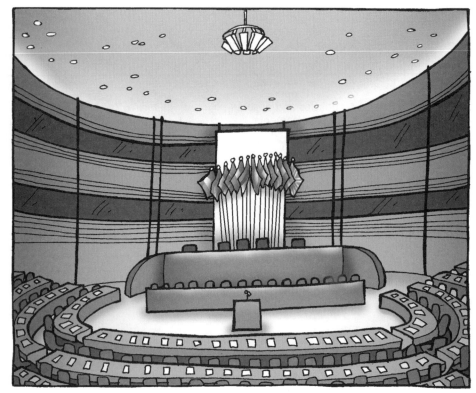

The European Parliament

4 The role and composition of the European Court of Justice

The European Union is one of the most powerful organizations in the world, with its own legal system. It therefore has its own court. The European Union's court is called the European Court of Justice (ECJ).

The ECJ has two main aims:

● to see that European law is interpreted efficiently

● to see that European law is applied fairly and effectively.

The ECJ consists of fifteen judges. One judge comes from each member state. Nine other legal experts called Advocates General advise the judges.

The ECJ is not bound by its own previous decisions. This means that it is in a position to 'create new law'. Its decisions are binding on all other courts in the European Union – they have to follow the rulings of the ECJ. Its ability to avoid following its own past decisions gives it a flexibility that is similar to that given to our own House of Lords by the **Practice Statement 1966**. This allows the House of Lords to avoid its past decisions. Without the flexibility to put aside old rulings, legislation would become stale and out of date.

Revision checklist

1 The European Union is a group of 15 powerful European countries who are moving together politically, economically and legally.

2 The main lawmaking body is the Council of Ministers. They vote on decisions.

3 Each country's vote relates to its size. This is called *weighted* voting.

4 The Committee of Permanent Representatives does most of the work when Ministers are not there.

5 The Commission is made up of representatives from all European member states, who look after the interests of the European Union rather than of their own country.

6 The Commission proposes policies and investigates the behaviour of large businesses in the EU.

7 The European Parliament's job is to discuss legislation and comment. It does not vote on legislation. This is the job of the Council.

8 The Parliament can investigate Ministers of the Council and dismiss the Commission.

9 The European Court of Justice (ECJ) is responsible for interpreting EU law and applying it.

10 The ECJ is not bound by its own previous decisions. It can create law in the form of its rulings.

Quick revision questions

1 What is the European Union?

2 What does the Council of Ministers do?

3 What does weighting do?

4 What do the Foreign Ministers do within the Council?

5 Whose interests do the Commissioners look after?

6 What are the key jobs of the Commission?

7 What powers has the European Parliament got?

8 What is the job of the European Court of Justice (ECJ)?

9 How does the ECJ create law?

10 How many judges sit on the ECJ?

Exam question

1 **a** What is the role of the following European institutions: [20 marks[
- the Council of Ministers
- the European Parliament
- the European Court of Justice?

     b Is the system of lawmaking in the European Union an effective one in terms of accountability? [25 marks]

Exam answer guide

1 **a** The following points can be used as a guide:

     ✓ The Council of Ministers is the key decision-making body of the EU. It votes on legislation which is suggested to it by the European Commission.

     ✓ The European Parliament discusses and comments on the legislation passed to it by the Commission. The Commission and the Council of Ministers are not bound by the views of the Parliament, but they take them seriously. The Parliament has power to make life difficult for the Commission and can investigate Ministers in the Council.

     ✓ The European Court of Justice interprets and applies European law. It is not bound by its own past decisions. Its findings are binding on all courts in the European Union.

     b Although the Parliament has no voting powers, the Ministers from each member state have. They are democratically elected, so have the backing of the voters at home. The Parliament has the power to investigate (the Ministers) and dismiss (The Commission), so it has some teeth. Checks and balances are in place to stop any of the elements from getting too powerful and abusing their power. Each element is accountable (i.e. has to answer) to someone.

UNIT 7

Primary and secondary sources of European law

Key points

1 Treaties and regulations
2 Directives and decisions
3 Implementation by the courts
4 Impact of European Union law on domestic institutions and law.

Why do I need to know about primary and secondary sources of European law?

Questions on this area often ask whether European or English law takes priority when there is a conflict. You will need to know the main sources of European law and how they are handled within the English legal system. There are some key cases which you will need to learn and quote to show your understanding.

Sources of European law

Answers to questions about the European Union and its legal system need to be balanced and thoughtful. Show both sides of the argument at all times.

1 Treaties and regulations

Treaties of the European Union

These are the main sources of European law. Essentially they are important agreements made by the member states. Treaties give power to the various institutions within the European Union and set the direction for the European Union to follow. They define the rights and responsibilities of member states. There are four main treaties.

- The Treaty of Rome (1957) essentially formed what is now called the European Union and established its legal status.
- The Maastricht Treaty (1992) explored further integration.
- The Amsterdam Treaty (1997) extended the work of Maastricht.
- The Nice Treaty (2000) explored the possibilities and issues surrounding enlargement of the European Union.

Much of the fine print of the treaties needs to be put in place before it has an effect. Regulations and directives are used to fill in the gaps.

Web activity

Go to the European Union website and explore the aims of the treaties mentioned.

Legal case: *Macarthys v Smith (1980)*

Article 119 of the Treaty of Rome says: 'men and women shall receive equal pay for equal work'. The woman in this case was able to claim her rights under the article since a previous male worker had been paid more for doing the same job.

Regulations

Regulations are rules which must automatically be obeyed by all member states. They are created under Article 249 of the Treaty of Rome (1957). They ensure consistency throughout the European Union since every country has to obey the same regulations. Regulations can be used against the state and against other individuals for protection of rights.

2 Directives and decisions

Directives

Directives lay down goals. It is up to each member state to decide how best to achieve the goals. The United Kingdom Government normally uses delegated legislation to meet the requirements of European directives.

Directives often fill in the detail of a treaty to make the law effective. This can be seen in *Van Duyn v Home Office (1975)*, which illustrates the power of directives in fine tuning provisions laid down by treaties. Member states are given a time limit for implementation. If this expires, the directive can still be used against the state (vertical), but cannot be used against other individuals (horizontal). If an individual has been put in an unfavourable position because a directive has not been implemented, they can sue the state for compensation.

Legal case: *Van Duyn v Home Office (1975)*

The Home Office banned Miss Van Duyn from the UK because she was a member of the Church of Scientology. Miss Van Duyn felt this went against her rights under treaty provisions which allowed free movement of European workers. A directive 64/221 specified, however, that the UK Government had a right to ban her if they felt her personal conduct was inappropriate. The Home Office won the case when the European Court of Justice gave their ruling.

Exam tip

Spend some time making sure that you understand the differences between the various European institutions.

Decisions

Decisions are normally directed at specific member states, individuals or companies. They are often used in the area of competition policy when the Commission has decided that this policy has been breached. Decisions are frequently made using articles 81 and 82 of the Treaty of Rome (1957).

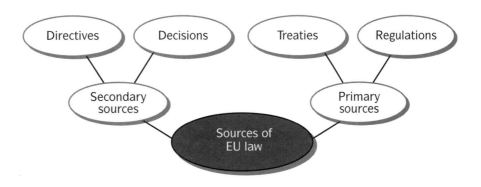

Sources of European law

3 Implementation by the courts

Directly applicable

A legal action or defence involving a provision of European Law can be brought in a national court if it is directly applicable. This means that the provision is automatically part of the national law of each member state. Individual member states do not have to go through a legislative process to make a directly applicable piece of legislation enforceable.

Direct effect

A piece of legislation is directly effective if it creates individual rights which can be enforced in the national courts. There are two types of direct effects.

- Vertical direct effects create rights against the state.
- Horizontal direct effects create rights against other individuals.

The English courts must enforce all of these laws and provisions. Furthermore, domestic English courts now have a duty to implement EU law in preference to English law.

> **Quick questions**
>
> What do the following terms mean: directly applicable, direct effect, vertical direct effect, horizontal direct effect?

4 Impact of European Union law on domestic institutions and law

The law of the European Union takes priority over the law of individual member states. *Van Gend en Loos v Netherlands (1962)* paved the way for this position.

Legal case: *Van Gend en Loos v Netherlands (1962)*

The Government of the Netherlands attempted to introduce new customs duties. A ruling by the European Court of Justice prevented this from happening, and in doing so established the supremacy of EU law over national law.

The **European Communities Act 1972** states that law created by the European Union immediately becomes English law. This means that lawmaking bodies such as the European Commission can propose laws that are applicable in the UK. Any disputes about these laws are eventually sorted out by the European Court of Justice. If the UK Parliament were to pass law that went directly against EU law, the ECJ would find the UK in breach of its duties and take appropriate action.

A second important case illustrated the view of the English Courts in relation to legislation that came into conflict with Europe.

Old barriers to EU supremacy

Legal case: *Factortame v Secretary of State (1991)*

The European Court of Justice ordered the House of Lords (the highest court in the English legal system) to suspend the operation of the **Merchant Shipping Act 1988** since it had come into conflict with articles of the Treaty of Rome (1957). The House of Lords obeyed the ruling and thereby acknowledged the supremacy of the ECJ over the House of Lords.

Group activity

What benefits does the UK receive from having a strong European Court of Justice?

Revision checklist

1 Treaties are the primary source of European law.

2 Treaties give power to the institutions of the European Union and set the direction for the whole system.

3 Examples of treaties include Rome, Maastricht, Amsterdam and Nice.

4 Regulations are also primary sources of law. They are rules which must be obeyed by all member states.

5 Directives are secondary sources of European law. They lay down goals to be reached. Member states have some flexibility about how to get there. The UK uses delegated legislation.

6 Decisions are also secondary sources. They are aimed at specific member states, institutions or individuals.

7 Directly applicable legislation automatically becomes law in all member states.

8 A vertical direct effect creates rights against the state. A horizontal direct effect creates rights against other individuals.

9 European law takes priority over English law: EU law is supreme.

10 The **European Communities Act 1972** brought the UK into the EU and established the supremacy of EU law over English law.

Quick revision questions

1 What is the power of a *treaty*?

2 Name four European treaties.

3 What is a *regulation*?

4 What is a *directive*?

5 Who does a *decision* relate to?

6 What is meant by *directly applicable*?

7 What is the difference between direct vertical and direct horizontal effects?

8 What legal case underlined the supremacy of EU law?

9 What is the **European Communities Act 1972**?

10 Where do cases go to after the House of Lords?

Exam question

1   **a** What are key sources of EU law? [20 marks]

    b What effect has membership of the EU had on our legal system?
    [25 marks]

Answer guide

1   **a** Key sources of EU legal power are:

    ✓ Treaties

    ✓ Regulations

    ✓ Directives

    ✓ Decisions.

    b The main effects of EU membership on the legal system have been the
replacement of English law with EU law when there is a conflict. EU law
takes priority and is supreme. We can use the European Court of Justice
when we are not sure of the correct interpretation of EU law, which in
some ways reduces the power of the Law Lords to explain the objectives
of legislation. The **European Communities Act 1972** meant that the UK
signed up to all the laws of the European Union before and after that
date.

Impetus for law reform

Key points

1 The role of Parliament
2 The role of judges
3 Effect of public opinion and pressure groups

Why do I need to know about impetus for law reform?

Questions on law reform will expect you to know the key players and how they operate. The independence of the judiciary makes them less likely to respond to pressure, whereas an elected Government is mindful of the next election. An understanding of this unit will help you with questions on how the legislative system works and will give you an insight into the dynamic nature of the legal world. It is important to look also at Module 2 Unit 1 on the Judiciary, Module 3 Unit 1 on Judicial precedent, Unit 3 on Acts of Parliament and Unit 9 on Law reform agencies.

'We want change!'

Glossary

The voters are technically called **constituents** and the area an MP represents is called the **constituency**.

Did you know?

You cannot vote in British elections if you are mentally incapable, a prisoner, have failed to put your name on the electoral register or you are the Queen.

1 The role of Parliament

The United Kingdom Parliament is made up of over 650 Members of Parliament. MPs are elected by voters, or **constituents**, who live in the area, or **constituency**, the MP represents.

During an election campaign political parties lay out their proposals for change in a document called a manifesto. The party elected by the people is under some obligation to meet its manifesto promises. Parliament's job is to make sure the Government carries out the wishes of the people. It is there to support the Government by voting for it, but it also questions Government proposals to make sure that the legislation eventually passed is correct and effective. Parliament scrutinizes legislation, that is, it looks at it in detail to make sure it is in order.

The examination of potential legislation occurs in the main chambers of the House of Commons and the House of Lords, and also in smaller sessions called Committees. A Committee is formed when a number of MPs come together in a group to look in more detail at the items suggested by the Government. Look back at Module 3 Unit 3 for more information.

Main institutions in the system

Political parties

The vast majority of MPs belong to a political party. They might be members of the Labour Party, the Conservative Party, the Liberal Democratic Party, or of any of the other smaller political parties. The political parties have different views about which laws should be passed and how the country should be run. The party with the most MPs normally has its way over what happens in Parliament. The leader of the Labour Party has significantly more MPs than any other party. Therefore the Labour Party normally wins any votes in the House of Commons over what laws should be passed. The party with the most MPs forms the Government and chooses the Prime Minister.

Did you know?

A Minister without Portfolio can be a member of the Cabinet but cannot be a member of the House of Commons.

The Cabinet

The Prime Minister selects the Cabinet as his or her working team. Members of the Cabinet are normally MPs. They are the heart of the Government, representing the key power inside the political system.

The Cabinet is the group of most senior and powerful elected Members of Parliament in the winning political party The Cabinet proposes legislation by putting forward a document called a bill. A bill is like a draft copy of an Act of Parliament. It is used for discussion purposes. It must go through a number of stages before it becomes law (see Unit 3-3). If the Prime Minister and the Cabinet support the bill, it has an excellent chance of becoming law.

The Government

The Government is formed by the party which wins the most seats in the general election. The Queen invites the leader of the party who has the most MPs to form the new Government, i.e. to take charge of the country and select the

Cabinet. The Prime Minister now forms 'her Majesty's Government'. In theory the Queen could refuse to make the leader of the largest party the Prime Minister. In reality this never happens.

The House of Commons

The House of Commons is the main debating chamber for the elected Members of Parliament. The majority political party, currently Labour, sits on one side facing the official Opposition, which is the party with the next highest number of MPs, at present the Conservatives. It is like a contest, with one side continually fighting the other over most issues. This system of aggressive examination of everything the other side says is known as *adversarial*.

The House of Lords

In addition to the elected House of Commons, there is another part to the parliamentary system called the House of Lords. In theory the Lords have a say in what legislation is passed and what is not, although in reality the most they can do is pass amendments and slow legislation down. Members of the House of Lords see themselves as a revising chamber. This means looking once again at legislation and improving parts which may have been missed in drafting or in the House of Commons. The system and mood in the House of Lords are much less aggressive but no less sharp.

A committee of the House of Lords also acts as the final appeal court within the English legal system, but looks at points of law rather than the details of the case itself. The Law Lords fulfil this function.

The Crown

The power of the monarch is still seen today in the power of the Crown to pass or reject legislation, in theory at least. The monarch has to give permission for any Act of Parliament to be put into force. This is known as Royal Assent. In the real world the Queen would never refuse to sign a bill. It is a mere formality. Just as the English legal system would never really want a showdown with the European Court of Justice, the Queen would have no benefit in confronting the elected House of Parliament. A delicate balance of power exists in the system.

2 The role of judges

We have seen that judges play a vital part in interpreting the law, and even in creating it

Judges are keen not to tread on the toes of Parliament/Government. In fact, they often state that they are trying to uphold the position of the Parliament/Government rather than trying to compete with it. They are, however, faced with the practical problems of their actions. What they decide will have implications for public policy and the actions of ordinary people, organizations and even Government departments and local authorities in the future.

Did you know?

The present Government has introduced a number of changes to reduce the power of the House of Lords and modernize its procedures.

Did you know?

The **Parliament Acts 1911** and **1949** mean that legislation passed in the House of Commons will become law even if the House of Lords does not like it. The most they can do is delay its passage.

Did you know?

The last time a monarch refused a piece of legislation which had been passed by the Houses of Parliament was in 1707.

Quick questions

List the elements of the parliamentary system.

Lord Radcliffe, a famous Law Lord of the 1960s, said:

'It is unacceptable that there should be two independent sources of lawmaking at work at the same time'.

This careful line is one present-day judges try to steer, although at times it is very difficult.

3 Effect of public opinion and pressure groups

The House of Commons is under constant pressure to pass legislation. This pressure comes from a number of sources, including the groups below.

Political pressure groups

Groups within and outside Parliament mount political campaigns to get favourable legislation. MPs and those who have influence on Parliament are lobbied for their support. The topics are endless, but include the banning of landmines and the legalization of cannabis.

Professional lobbyists

The world of professional lobbyists started in the United States, but it is now well and truly part of our system. Specialists are hired by big businesses and organizations to put their points of view in the most effective way. The ethics of the methods used are sometimes very questionable.

Environmental groups

Pressure groups such as Greenpeace and Friends of the Earth have been incredibly successful in raising the issue of environmental damage. They skilfully put their message to the public by using sophisticated publicity stunts which the media uses as news. Legislation passed to date in the UK has been relatively weak, however. Forthcoming European legislation promises to be much more hard-hitting.

Research activity

Find out some more about the legal campaigns run by major pressure groups. Greenpeace and Friends of the Earth have very efficient press offices you can contact. Also use the Internet and your local library.

Penal reformers

Organizations such as The Howard League and National Association for the Rehabilitation of Offenders specialize in trying to improve the prison system and its aftercare facilities through changes in legislation.

Race and bureaucratic reform

Clearly, one of the most successful campaigns of recent years was based around the tragic death of Stephen Lawrence, a young black teenager from South-east London. The Macpherson Report investigated the murder and made many recommendations for change. Some of these related to the way whole institutions discriminate against ethnic minorities. The term 'institutionalized racism' was one used many times in the report.

Trade unions

Trade unions have had more influence with the Government since the re-election of a Labour Party. They now speak directly to the Prime Minister. Many MPs are sponsored by trade unions and will speak on topics affecting trade union members.

Visit activity

See if you can arrange a visit to a trade union office or have a representative come into your school/college. Try to get an idea of the areas of law that unions are interested in reforming.

The general public

One of the main problems we have is trying to identify who the general public are. We live in a rich and varied society, and so the concept of one 'general public' is complex. Opinion polls by political parties may indicate where the 'majority' of the public are on any one issue and popular legislation may follow.

The general public

The media

We live in a world where media influence is very powerful. Some say that it can even decide the outcome of elections. The Government is clearly affected by focused media pressure, such as that surrounding dangerous dogs, protection of children and even the way that judges give sentences to criminals.

Other groups

Other sources of pressure include charities, churches, big businesses, welfare organizations, consumer groups and dedicated individuals.

Research activity

Try to find some pages from *Hansard,* the official record of the Houses of Parliament. The Internet would be a good place to start. Identify the various lines of argument taken by different speakers.

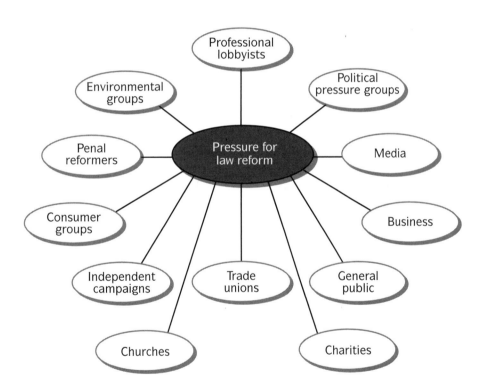

Who wants law reform?

Revision checklist

1 The UK Parliament is made up of over 650 MPs who vote on legislation.

2 One of the main jobs of Parliament is to examine legislation, whether in the main chamber or in Committee Rooms.

3 The main elements of the parliamentary system are: political parties, the Cabinet, the Government, the House of Commons, the House of Lords and the Crown.

4 The Queen must give her permission for a bill to become legislation. This is known as the Royal Assent.

5 Judges try to take a neutral stand.

6 Lord Radcliffe said that there should be only one source of law.

7 Pressure comes on the Houses of Parliament from: political pressure groups, lobbyists, environmental groups, penal reformers, campaign groups, trade unions, the media and the general public.

8 Political lobbyists are professionals who attempt to persuade MPs of the virtue of their client's case.

9 Trade unions influence Parliament by sponsoring MPs.

10 Pressure groups attempt to target the general public using media coverage.

Quick revision questions

1 Why do MPs want to support the development of law?

2 What does *scrutiny* mean?

3 What do members of the Cabinet do?

4 How does the House of Commons operate?

5 What is the main function of the House of Lords?

6 Does the Queen play a part in the development of law?

7 Why are judges careful when developing new law?

8 What are the main pressures on Parliament?

9 What does a political lobbyist do?

10 How do trade unions exert influence on Parliament?

Exam question

1 a Where do the main pressures for changes in the law come from?
[20 marks]

b Who should decide what laws are passed? [25 marks]

Exam answer guide

1 a Main pressures come from:
- ✓ MPs within Parliament
- ✓ Pressure groups and lobbyists
- ✓ Media sources
- ✓ General public
- ✓ Big businesses
- ✓ Churches and charities
- ✓ Welfare organizations
- ✓ Consumer groups
- ✓ Individuals and small groups.

b Who should make laws is a complex question. Possible answers include:
- ✓ MPs who represent the general public
- ✓ Cabinet on behalf of the country
- ✓ Government departments
- ✓ Local authorities
- ✓ Any from part **a** are worth considering.

Drafting law is a complex business and the present system at least consults widely on all legislation to be passed so that the credit or blame can be shared out.

Law reform agencies

Key points

1 The role of the Law Commission
2 Royal Commissions
3 Other agencies of law reform

What do I need to know about law reform agencies?

Questions on law reform will link to judicial precedent and Parliamentary lawmaking. The whole legal system is a mix of solid predictable legislation and built-in flexibility for a society that is changing fast. You will need to understand where the pressure for change comes from (see Module 3 Unit 8) and how the system can respond. Insight into law reform agencies will give depth to other areas of your work.

New law is often needed

1 The role of the Law Commission

The Law Commission is an advisory body set up in 1965. It researches areas of law that could benefit from reform and produces draft bills for passage through Parliament. It was part of the Government's plan to 'modernize' Britain. It is the only full-time permanent Government-funded organization that investigates and comments on law reform. English law is a combination of statute law and common law, some of which goes back a very long time. The Law Commission's job is to 'keep under review all the law with a view to its systematic development'. The Lord Chancellor's Department often refers areas of law that it wants explored to the Law Commission.

The work of law reform is ultimately the concern of Parliament, but the Law Commission provides useful research and ideas which contribute to debate on legal issues. The Commission consults widely on issues of concern and has five full-time officials who coordinate the information and put it into an effective vehicle for change. The Commission does not offer legal advice to individuals or organizations, but is concerned with wider legal issues.

The organization is made up of people from the legal profession. It includes a High Court Judge, a QC, a solicitor and two legal academics. The Commission is also supported by a range of administrative staff, including Parliamentary Counsel who draft Government bills.

Index card revision

Using index cards, list the main figures in the Law Commission.

The Law Commission

Work of the Law Commission

The Law Commission works on about 20 or 30 projects at any one time. A project will attempt to identify any defects in the current system and then look for possible solutions. It may possibly look at how foreign legal systems deal with similar issues.

In its first 25 years, the Law Commission produced 100 reports. Over 70 per cent of these resulted in legislation.

There are five key areas of concern for the Law Commission:

- the development and reform of law
- getting rid of outdated law (repealing obsolete law)
- the simplification of the law
- codifying the law (putting it all in one place)
- getting rid of laws that conflict with each other.

Group activity

1 Can you think of any areas of law which you think might benefit from reform?

2 Who would you ask for their opinions on the issue?

2 Royal Commissions

When an area of law causes public concern, a Royal Commission is often set up. A Royal Commission is made up of a large cross-section of people. All have an interest in the issue explored, but most are not legally qualified.

The Commission undertakes research, interviews relevant parties, and then publishes a report. Parliament is under no obligation to act on the recommendations of a Royal Commission, even though the process may take many months or even years to complete and represent innovative and valuable contributions to the area under investigation.

- The Royal Commission on Police Procedure in 1981 had many of its recommendations incorporated into the **Police and Criminal Evidence Act 1984 (PACE)**.
- The Royal Commission on Civil Liability and Compensation in 1978 investigated awards for medical care and social security benefits.
- The Royal Commission on Justices of the Peace in 1948 was one of the first and most revealing investigations into the backgrounds of lay magistrates.

Agencies for law reform

3 Other agencies of law reform

Independent pressure groups

A number of high-profile groups focus on particular areas of the law to bring about change and improvement. One example of this is the campaigning group Liberty.

This particular campaigning group uses its resources to oppose or modify legislative changes which it believes may reduce our civil liberties and freedoms. Liberty has been in the forefront of pressures to bring about freedom of information laws and has bitterly opposed the ending of the 'right to silence' and changes planned for the curbing of right to trial by jury.

Web activity

Look for Liberty's website at www.liberty.org.uk. What are their current areas of interest?

Public inquiries

Public inquiries are often set up after high-profile disasters. They often lead to changes in the law to prevent a repeat of the event.

Public inquiry into the BSE crisis

This inquiry looked at the possible reasons for the spread of the disease amongst cattle, and its transfer to humans in the form of new variant CJD.

Public inquiry into the Hillsborough disaster

This inquiry looked at the circumstances surrounding the tragic deaths of football fans in the Hillsborough stadium in Sheffield, including the design of the ground and policing methods.

Public inquiry into Alder Hey Children's Hospital

Doctors at Alder Hey Children's Hospital in Liverpool kept organs of dead children for research purposes, without asking or telling the children's parents.

Public inquiry into Paddington train crash

The troubles on the railway system have caused a series of high-profile crashes in which passengers and train crew have died. The inquiry looked not only at the events on the day but the reasons behind the incident.

Public inquiries are designed to get behind the facts and attempt to provide information to stop the same circumstances arising again. They have no power to implement their proposals. It is for the Government to consider them and to respond.

Group activity

1   Public inquiries are designed to get at the truth and stop similar disasters. What obstacles may prevent the implementation of recommendations?

Law Reform Committee

This is a small part-time committee which focuses on specialized areas needing technical legal solutions. It was formed in 1952 and is still at times consulted by the Law Commission. The Lord Chancellor refers work to it occasionally. It is involved only with civil law.

The Criminal Law Revision Committee

This committee plays a similar role to the Law Reform Committee, but in the criminal law field. The **Theft Acts** are its main area of success. As with the Law Reform Committee, this is a part-time group.

Revision checklist

1 The Law Commission was created in 1965 to modernize the systems of law in Britain.

2 The Law Commission produces draft bills to go through Parliament.

3 The Law Commission's job is to 'review' and 'develop' law.

4 The Commission is involved with wide legal issues and does not give specific legal advice to individuals.

5 The Commission is made up of a High Court Judge, a QC, a solicitor and two legal academics.

6 The Law Commission has a good success rate for turning drafts into legislation.

7 Royal Commissions are set up by Government to explore an area of public concern. They involve a wide cross-section of people.

8 A number of pressure groups, such as Liberty, try to change legislation.

9 Public inquiries are set up to investigate serious incidents or circumstances which normally have led to the loss of life.

10 Two part-time bodies also look at law reform: the Law Reform Committee and the Criminal Law Revision Committee.

Quick revision questions

1 What are the main jobs of the Law Commission?

2 Who gives it its work?

3 Who are the main members of the Law Commission?

4 How successful has the Law Commission been?

5 Who is normally in charge of a Royal Commission?

6 How does a Royal Commission do its work?

7 Name some examples of Royal Commissions.

8 What kinds of areas come under the investigation of public inquiries?

9 What is the main work of the Law Reform Committee?

10 What is the main work of the Criminal Law Revision Committee?

1   **a** What is the main work of the Law Commission? [20 marks]

    b Has the Law Commission been successful in its work since 1965?
      [25 marks]

Exam answer guide

1   **a** Main work includes:
    ✓ Reforming the law
    ✓ Developing the law
    ✓ Simplifying the law
    ✓ Making the law sensible.

    b The work of the Law Commission has been successful in some areas.
They have done a good job in reforming specific legal areas and getting
rid of old laws. In terms of making the law system simpler, there is a long
way to go. We still have a huge mixture of common law and statute law
from Parliament.

Table of Acts of Parliament

Abortion Act 1967
Access to Justice Act 1999
Act of Settlement 1700
Arbitration Act 1996
Attachment of Earnings Act 1971
Bail Act 1976
Bail (Amendment) Act 1993
Channel Tunnel Act 1986
Civil Procedure Act 1997
Civil Procedures Rules 1999
Court and Legal Services Act 1990
Courts Act 1971
Crime (Sentences) Act 1997
Crime and Disorder Act 1998
Criminal Justice Act 1982
Criminal Justice Act 1988
Criminal Justice Act 1993
Emergency Powers Act 1920
Employment Act 1996
European Communities Act 1972
Finance Act 1976
Human Rights Act 1998
Interpretation Act 1978
Magistrates' Courts Act 1980
Mental Health Act 1983
Merchant Shipping Act 1988
Misuse of Drugs Act 1971
Murder (abolition of death penalty) Act 1965
Parliament Act 1911
Parliament Act 1949
Police and Criminal Evidence Act 1984
Powers of Criminal Courts (Sentencing) Act 2000
Practice Statement 1966
Prosecution of Offences Act 1985
Public Order Act 1986
Race Relations Act 1976
Royal Assent Act 1961
Social Security Act 1984
Theft Act 1968

Table of legal cases

Addie v Dumbreck (1929)
British Railways Board v Herrington (1972)
Daniels v White (1938)
Donoghue v Stevenson (1932)
Hall v Simons (2000)
Heydon's Case (1584)
Levi v Tesco (2001)
London Tramways v London County Council (1898)
Macarthys v Smith (1980)
Osman v DPP (1999)
Pepper v Hart (1993)
R v Allen (1872)
R v Field (2001)
R v Pinochet (1998)
R v R (1991)
Rondel v Worsley (1969)
Royal College of Nursing v Department of Health and Social Security (1981)
Scott v Avery (1855)
Smith v Hughes (1960)
Tanfern Ltd v Cameron-MacDonald (2000)
Van Duyn v Home Office (1975)
Van Gend en Loos v Netherlands (1962)
Young v Bristol Aeroplane Company (1944)

Index

If you've liked this, you'll also like this!

A2 Law for OCR

Having used this book for AS Law you'll have seen how well it covers all the information you need for your course.

A2 Law for OCR is written by the same author and follows the same winning format as the AS book.

- It is OCR specific so it will cover only material relevant to your A2 course.

- Exam tips and practice questions are provided throughout will make sure you are fully prepared for the exam.

- Summary boxes, glossaries and exam questions help make studying easier.

Why not order a copy of *A2 Law for OCR* today?

You can contact us direct on:

(t) *01865 888068*   **(f)** *01865 314029*

(e) *orders@heinemann.co.uk*   **(w)** *www.heinemann.co.uk*